**FILM STARS**

Stars are an integral part of every major film industry in the world. In this pivotal new series, each book is devoted to an international movie star, looking at the development of their identity, their acting and performance methods, the cultural significance of their work, and their influence and legacy. Taking a wide range of different stars, including George Clooney, Brigitte Bardot and Dirk Bogarde among others, this series encompasses the sphere of silent and sound acting, Hollywood and non-Hollywood areas of cinema, and child and adult forms of stardom. With its broad range, but a focus throughout on the national and historical dimensions to film, the series offers students and researchers a new approach to studying film.

**SERIES EDITORS**
Martin Shingler and Susan Smith

T0348019

# Tony LEUNG
# CHIU-Wai

MARK GALLAGHER

A BFI book published by Palgrave

First published 2018 by
**PALGRAVE**

on behalf of the

**BRITISH FILM INSTITUTE**
21 Stephen Street, London, W1T 1LN
www.bfi.org.uk

Palgrave in the UK is an imprint of Macmillan Publishers Limited,
registered in England, company number 785998, of 4 Crinan Street,
London, N1 9XW.

Palgrave® and Macmillan® are registered trademarks in the United States,
the United Kingdom, Europe and other countries.

ISBN   978 1 84457 781 1
eISBN 978 1 83902 094 0
ePDF  978 1 84457 783 5

A catalogue record for this book is available from the British Library.

A catalog record for this book is available from the Library of Congress.

Cover image: Entertainment Pictures / Alamy Stock Photo

# CONTENTS

# ACKNOWLEDGEMENTS

Eternal thanks to friends and colleagues near and far who provided kinship, solace and laughter, and generally tolerated my presence, including Kevin Gallagher, Karen Eng, Andy Deck, Paul Jenner, Elaine Roth, Paul McDonald, Aron Golden and Lisa Schultz, Michael Pebworth and Lindsay Schubert, Nate Nichols and Fran Salafia, Seth Friedman and Luci Hackbert, Peter and Cindy Witkow, Iain Smith and Cai Edwards, Matt Sosnow and Sara Trilling, Edward Jones, Bernard Radfar, Jon Burgerman, Nuno Jorge and Brad Prager. For their inspiring scholarship and mutual interest in East Asian cinema, and for sharing Tony Leung lore, thanks to Chi-Yun Shin, Lin Feng, Sabrina Yu, Luke Robinson and Victor Fan. Thanks too to Kathleen Rowe Karlyn for fostering my academic interest in screen stardom, and to Rikke Schubart and Chris Holmlund for furthering it with intellectual support, cheerleading and plenty more. Thanks also to all my colleagues at Nottingham, especially Paul Grainge, Roberta Pearson, Gianluca Sergi, Paul Gladston and Stephanie Lewthwaite. Thanks as well to Gina Marchetti and Aaron Magnan-Park at the University of Hong Kong, Gary Bettinson at Lancaster University, Yannis Tzioumakis at the University of Liverpool and Lydia Papadimitriou at Liverpool John Moores University, and Nick Rees-Roberts and Catherine O'Rawe at the University of Bristol for speaking invitations, collegiality and fellowship. My gratitude also goes to the University of Nottingham's Centre for Contemporary

East Asian Cultural Studies for research support, to Nicola Cattini and Sophia Contento at Palgrave and BFI Publishing for valuable editorial and production assistance, and to series editors Martin Shingler and Susan Smith for their support and stewardship of this project from its inception.

Portions of this book were previously published in different form. An earlier version of Chapter 1 appeared as 'Tony Leung Chiu-Wai: Acting Sexy in Hong Kong and China' in *Asian Cinema* vol. 27 no. 1 (2016), and Chapter 4 adapts material from 'Tony Leung's Thrillers and Transnational Stardom' (in *East Asian Film Noir*, eds Chi-Yun Shin and Mark Gallagher [2015]) and '"Would You Rather Spend More Time Making Serious Cinema?": *Hero* and Tony Leung's Polysemic Masculinity' (in *Global Chinese Cinema: The Culture and Politics of 'Hero'*, eds Gary Rawnsley and Ming-Yeh Rawnsley [2010]). Thanks to the editors for their permission to include this material.

Finally, special thanks to Melissa Li for warmth and support of all kinds, not least for weathering a marathon viewing of *Red Cliff*. I'll never be a Tony Leung–calibre romantic lead, but Melissa has made me feel like one.

# INTRODUCTION

In the flourishing of academic work on film stars and actors both before and following the 1979 publication of Richard Dyer's pioneering book *Stars*, stars of Hollywood and European cinemas have dominated research. This emphasis has reflected scholars' cultural origins and predilections as well as the types of films and film discourse circulating most widely in global culture. The world of screen stardom is far vaster than that encompassed by Euro-American cultures and scholarship, though. Seeking to contribute to ongoing English-language scholarship on global acting and stardom, I have been thrilled to be given the opportunity to research and to write at length about Tony Leung Chiu-Wai (梁朝偉, aka Zhaowei Liang), a contemporary Chinese male star in the midst of an exceptional and varied screen career.[1]

This short monograph joins the work of scholars such as those featured in Mary Farquhar and Yingjin Zhang's 2011 anthology *Chinese Film Stars* and Leung Wing-Fai and Andy Willis's 2014 collection *East Asian Film Stars*, as well as longer monographs on stars such as Anna May Wong (from Graham Russell Gao Hodges 2004), Jet Li (from Sabrina Qiong Yu 2012a) and Chow Yun-Fat (from Lin Feng 2017). This modest volume builds on the methods of these scholars as well as those working more broadly in star and performance studies and in East Asian film and culture. It investigates the performances and career of film (and previously, television) star Leung in ways that I hope illuminate at least three areas of intellectual interest.

The first is film stardom in China and East Asia, tracing the specific dynamics of stardom in Hong Kong, mainland China and the East Asian region. Among other subjects, I address the importance of television series in Hong Kong for training screen actors and incubating local popularity to foster subsequent film stardom. Following Leung Wing-Fai, I also approach the phenomenon of transmedia stardom in Hong Kong and East Asia, with stars routinely crossing television, film and popular music. Finally in this area, I consider intra-regional circulation, including cultural and political considerations as actors move among different East Asian production environments.

Second, the book intervenes into debates around transnational and global stardom. I consider, for example, reception of star performance as it moves beyond indigenous cultural, industrial and linguistic contexts. Relatedly, I highlight stars' varying reputations in different locations, specifically Leung Chiu-Wai's reputation as a comic and *wuxia pian* actor in Hong Kong and China but as an art-cinema figure elsewhere, particularly in the US and Europe. As such, I study too the discursive formations that arise in different regions and film cultures, including the international reception of stars in terms of paradigmatic roles rather than through access to transmedia activity and local extratextual discourses such as publicity and star gossip. Here too, I reflect on gender, race and ethnicity as framed textually, as well as in distinct production contexts and varying reception conditions.

Third, this book researches genre-based stardom and actor–director collaborations, addressing global stardom's connections to internationally circulating film genres and to acclaimed directors. I consider stars' roles as generic markers to distinguish films in the expansive global marketplace, and genres' parallel roles in providing a coherent platform for circulation of discrete performances across a diverse filmography. In this context, I stress film stars' affiliations with acclaimed, 'festival darling' directors – for Leung, directors such as Wong Kar-Wai, Ang Lee and Hou Hsiao-Hsien – and the related phenomenon of stars' festival presence as means to build reputations based on artistic collaboration.

This book's overall argument is that Leung is a flexible, mobile and durable screen actor and star. His nearly 100 roles in television dramas and popular and speciality film features spanning genres and modes attest to his flexibility as a performer. Meanwhile, his mobility is evident in his cross-media work and stardom – bridging film, television and popular music – as well as the geographic mobility of his work, which has taken him to disparate East Asian production environments and finds his work and image circulating worldwide in theatrical exhibition, at film festivals and on home video. This mobility renders him by turns a local Hong Kong star, a Chinese star and a transnational star, both regionally in East and Southeast Asia and globally. Finally, his thirty-five years and counting of screen acting – from television roles with demanding production schedules in his early adulthood, to prolific film acting across the 1980s and 1990s, and continuing to ongoing roles in major East Asian features in his mid-fifties – along with the persistence of his reputation as a dramatic actor, popular star and successful musician, testify to his durability. Leung's career therefore illuminates transmedia and transnational screen labour; opportunities for mobility in regional and global screen industries; circuits of distribution, promotion and discourse along which stars' work and reputations travel; and screen actors' negotiations among shifting industries, political systems and popular tastes from the 1980s to present.

Leung's career demonstrates ways East Asian media industries make use of creative labour across media, genres and producing nations. A native Cantonese speaker, he has played roles in Mandarin and Vietnamese and acted in films with co-stars speaking Korean and Japanese (and while fluent in English, he has not played an English-language role). Among his more than seventy feature-film roles to date, he has worked in productions for industries housed in Hong Kong, Taiwan, mainland China and Vietnam, and some of his films have involved French and US production capital as well. Companies financing Leung's films include Media Asia (Hong Kong producer of films including the *Infernal Affairs* [2002–3] and *Tokyo Raiders/Seoul Raiders* [2000, 2005] series), Paradis Films and Orly Films (French co-producers, alongside other companies, of *2046* [2004]), Block 2 and Jet Tone Productions (Hong Kong co-producers of many films from director Wong Kar-Wai, the latter company co-founded by Wong) and many others. The co-production *Cyclo* (1995), for example, puts Leung under the aegis of eight distinct French production entities, including the international brand Canal+ and the Société Française de Production (SFP), which funds mostly French television efforts. Similarly, the credits for *2046*, with Leung in the lead role, list twelve separate production companies from seven countries in North America, Western Europe and East Asia. The lavish historical epic *Red Cliff* (2008–9) pairs him again with frequent Taiwanese-Japanese co-star Takeshi Kaneshiro and lists production companies housed in mainland China, Hong Kong, Taiwan, South Korea and Japan, further attesting to transnational investment in Leung's continued stardom.

Among male stars not associated primarily with action roles, Leung is Chinese diasporic cinema's most successful contemporary transnational star. (In the other category, action stars Jackie Chan, Jet Li and Chow Yun-Fat have long commanded greater international recognition than does Leung, as has the American-born Donnie Yen in recent years.) Awareness of Leung is partly complicated by the presence of two prominent Tony Leungs – Tony Leung Chiu-Wai and Tony Leung Ka-Fai – as actors in transnational cinema originating in greater China, compounded by the fact that the men have appeared in many similar films, and even starred together in international releases such as 1994's *Ashes of Time* as well as numerous local Hong Kong films. Hong Kong audiences have long distinguished the two Leungs through their marked height difference, and thus the nicknames 'Big Tony' and 'Little Tony'. The star persona of the diminutive but globally better-known 'Little Tony' shows remarkable portability across genres, national cinemas and production contexts.

Born in Hong Kong in 1962, Leung Chiu-Wai has since the late 1980s earned visibility in a range of regionally produced, internationally distributed art and popular films, including such films as *Hard-Boiled* (1992), *Chungking Express* (1994), *Hero* (2002) and *Lust, Caution* (2007). Leung's initial success as a television actor on Hong Kong's TVB network strongly defined him as a local star. In the ensuing decades, Hong Kong's film industry has consistently promoted and commemorated him, for example, by regularly nominating him for acting prizes at the annual Hong Kong Film Awards. Even as Leung has participated in successful Hong Kong productions such as the industry-reviving *Infernal Affairs* (2002), he has starred too in numerous co-productions with mainland Chinese companies, ranging from the global hit *Hero* to the regional success *Lust, Caution*. Though the latter aroused controversy in China for its graphic sex scenes, Leung's mainland star status did not markedly suffer as a result. Indeed, his most recent roles have been in ideologically uncontroversial – or explicitly pro-state – mainland co-productions such as *Red Cliff*, *The Silent War* (2012) and *The Grandmaster* (2013).

Defined by the circulation of his films, their textual features and critical and popular responses, Leung figures varyingly as a local, regional or global star. Anchored by a Cannes Best Actor award for *In the Mood for Love* (2000), Leung's global reputation has depended strongly on his repeated collaborations with Wong Kar-Wai. His work in the past decade in Mandarin-language productions with mainland settings and locations newly establishes him as a mainland box-office attraction. This career path revises familiar trajectories of transnational stardom, but follows a similar economic logic, with China now attracting many Hong Kong, Korean, British and American stars thanks to its recent ascension to major production centre and release market.

Leung's career illuminates the nature of acting across film and television, in regional and international cinemas and in popular genres as well as expressly art-oriented filmmaking. Moreover, the different ways Leung has been promoted and received in local, regional and international contexts demonstrate both the fluidity of star reputation and the constraints imposed by distinct reception formations that call upon particular cultural knowledge (or in contrast, that lack access to that knowledge). Leung has enjoyed a reputation in Hong Kong and elsewhere in East Asia as a performer of diverse artistic, comic and physical talents. In the West, however, he has been understood chiefly as an art-cinema star, particularly through his multiple collaborations with Hong Kong filmmaker Wong, whose films prior to *The Grandmaster* gained greater critical and commercial success overseas than in Hong Kong or even across East Asia.

Leung's career also represents well the transmedial nature of Hong Kong stardom. While no longer active in television work, Leung has, like many fellow stars, pursued a parallel career as a pop singer, releasing a dozen albums from the mid-1980s to the mid-2000s. While this book devotes only modest attention to Leung's musical output, his singing career markedly informs his local and regional reputation and contributes to his status as a versatile talent, a prolific actor and entertainer thoroughly enmeshed in Hong Kong's and now China's major cultural industries.

Leung's acting ability and his expansive choices of roles offer a rich series of case studies through which to draw conclusions about contemporary Hong Kong, Chinese, pan-Asian and global stardom. By framing Leung as a dynamic cultural agent, I hope to raise questions too about the visibility and value of creative labour in a range of significant industrial formations. Given the striking changes that have occurred in Hong Kong's and mainland China's film industries since the 1980s, coupled with the varying climate of international film financing and distribution in the same period, and the new opportunities for diasporic and cross-cultural engagement made possible by technologies such as VCD, DVD and the Internet, Leung's activity across the period not only tells us much about East Asian or global stars but also provides a model for wider understandings of screen artistry and international cultural labour.

I organise this book into five chapters, each stressing particular facets of Leung's acting, stardom and appeal to critics or to screen consumers in general. Known for his good looks and sex appeal as well as his acting skill, Leung first merits attention, in Chapter 1, as a respectable East Asian sex symbol and as a romantically appealing Chinese man in international circulation and reception. Turning to Leung's early career, Chapter 2 considers how his acting style develops to suit the aesthetic and dramatic needs of Hong Kong television genres. Comparatively, it also investigates his parallel performances in 1980s and early 1990s Hong Kong cinema, spanning comic, dramatic and action roles. Chapter 3 approaches Leung as a particularly pan-Asian actor and star, tracing his move in the 1990s from local Hong Kong cinema to regional Asian productions. I show too how Leung's work across East Asian production contexts contributes to his growing reputation as a global art-cinema star, particularly through films' exhibition and promotion at key international festivals such as Cannes. Next, because Leung has worked repeatedly in numerous recognisable genres such as action, martial arts, comedy and thriller, Chapter 4 examines the dramatic and physical tools he uses to perform in genre films and argues for actors' transit across genres as a distinct feature of Hong Kong (and increasingly, of Chinese) stardom. Finally, Chapter 5 highlights Leung's work in the past decade in mainland Chinese films and China/Hong Kong co-productions. Addressing Chinese conceptions of star performance and of acting as cultural work, this last chapter studies the ongoing mainlandisation of cultural products that involve Hong Kong filmmakers and actors, focusing on aspects of Leung's most recent performances that encourage diverse viewer responses.

Overall, Leung's notable work in regionally and internationally successful popular and art cinemas since the 1980s makes him an ideal case through which to draw conclusions about the global dissemination and reception of Chinese screen art and popular culture. As a celebrated, contemporary screen and music performer, Leung has been active and visible in ways that allow us to gain new understandings of Chinese screen workers in local, regional and global cultural and industrial contexts. (And it has not hurt that he started out handsome and remains handsome.)

# 1 HOW TO ACT SEXY

Described by the Asian-American-themed magazine *Giant Robot* as looking 'like sex in a white suit' (Ko 2001: 37), Leung Chiu-Wai has since the early 1980s enjoyed a reputation as a sexually charismatic performer.[1] Much of his film work since the late 1980s, as well as some of his work in popular Hong Kong television series across that decade, has drawn on his good looks. And while mostly unknown in the US despite numerous international awards and prestige releases, Leung did earn a memorable notice as one of *People* magazine's 'Sexiest Men Alive' in 2000 (if as 'Sexiest Newcomer', despite his scores of prior film roles). Internationally distributed films such as *Chungking Express*, *In the Mood for Love*, and *Lust, Caution*, along with many Hong Kong romantic comedies, thrillers and martial-arts films, have capitalised on his physical appeal and his ability to perform as a sexually charismatic man.[2] In this chapter, I investigate Leung Chiu-Wai as a regional and global star, focusing on attributes of his acting that convey sex appeal or have been received as sexy. A lead actor in more than two dozen television series in the 1980s and 1990s in his native Hong Kong as well as scores of genre films, Leung has acquired an international reputation based on roles in art-cinema efforts from filmmakers such as Wong Kar-Wai, Ang Lee and Hou Hsiao-Hsien. Leung thus appears a popular star in a regional Asian context but a more rarefied, art-cinema performer internationally. Despite this bifurcated reputation, his sex appeal yields a powerful symbolic currency bankable in local as well as global contexts. Sex appeal also demonstrates Leung's flexibility as an actor. He performs both straight and gay romantic roles, alternately displays gentlemanliness or caddishness in romantic interactions, and plays characters ranging from sexually passive or de facto asexual figures to Lotharios and outright predators. Responses to his possible appeal are similarly flexible, registering in different ways in diverse reception contexts. Through attention to the highly legible yet difficult-to-quantify category of sex appeal, I identify features of Leung's acting and stardom that inform his overall career activity. By addressing a screen star's performance history and long-term creative trajectory, I begin here to account for the complex performative and cultural phenomenon of cinematic sex appeal. Sex appeal is far from the only lens through which to view Leung and his work, but it does correspond substantially to his star reputation and his screen work's reception.

Leung is arguably greater China's most acclaimed contemporary film actor, the recipient not only of the Cannes Film Festival's Best Actor award in 2001 for his lead role in *In the Mood for Love*, but also a four-time nominee and three-time winner of Best Actor prizes at Taiwan's annual Golden Horse Awards, a three-time winner of the Best Actor prize at the Hong Kong Film Critics Association's annual Golden Bauhinia Awards, and the winner of multiple other Asian and US festival awards. Most remarkably, since 1987 Leung has been nominated fourteen times as best actor or best supporting actor at the annual Hong Kong Film Awards, winning seven times. In 2008, he also won the Hong Kong Society of Cinematographers' annual 'Most Charismatic Actor' award.[3] This designation serves as a pivot point for one tool of my analysis, assessing Leung's on-screen charisma, which includes (though is not limited to) sex appeal. Leung has played various types across his more than thirty-five years of screen acting, from sexless, noble warrior or avatar of Zen philosophy to sweet seducer or amoral cad, with occasional detours such as mopey gay expatriate or sadistic revenger. Here, I explore in particular sex scenes and episodes of physical display in a series of Leung's films, some local Hong Kong films and others categorisable as global art-cinema works. Scenes in each offer explicit sites for the articulation of actorly charisma and sex appeal.

To approach sex appeal as a manifestation of charisma, I turn to Leslie O'Dell's model of the 'charismatic chameleon', proposed in her book of the same title. O'Dell argues that successful acting involves the interplay of charismatic and chameleonic properties. For her, charisma involves 'the unleashing of an intensely personal psychic energy' that 'fill[s] … fictional characters with a compelling spark of individuality' (2010: 4, xiii). Such energy combines with technical skill: 'Actors need to discipline their voices, bodies, and imagination so that they can adapt themselves, like the chameleon, to the fictional character they are portraying and to the world … in which that character appears' (2010: xiii). She notes further that 'a chameleon actor will demonstrate mastery of the means of expressive communication in voice, face, and body' (2010: 3). O'Dell offers her book in part as a training manual for actors. Leung's own training, in the early 1980s in the TVB television channel's actor-training programme, probably did not conform to O'Dell's approach. Still, the basic 'charismatic chameleon' template encourages us to identify in screen performances both consistent expressions of personal energy and chameleonesque adaptations to the dramatic requirements of given roles. The model thus gives us some purchase on manifestations of sex appeal, which can combine performers' individualised affects with specific character attributes, and which aspects of the cinematic apparatus such as framing and lighting can magnify or downplay. While sex appeal, like physical attractiveness generally, resists empirical analysis, textual evidence and extratextual materials such as industry awards, magazine covers and journalistic and other discourse indicate constructions of Leung as a sexually desirable figure in East Asian as well as wider global contexts.

# Lust and its tamer precursors

We can briefly return now to Leung's 'Most Charismatic Actor' award of 2008. The award represents a broad-brush assessment, not least because it has gone to a wide range of Hong Kong and Chinese leading men, men whose characterisations and performance styles lack common currency. Recipients in the past decade include Tony Leung Ka-Fai (in 2006), Aaron Kwok (2007), Donnie Yen (2009), Simon Yam (2010), Huang Xiaoming (2011), Lau Ching-Wan (2012), Nicolas Tse (2013), Louis Koo (2014) and Gordon Lam (2015), each winning the award through appearances in films ranging from historical martial-arts action and contemporary police thrillers to non-action dramas. While the award is not attached to specific films, for Leung Chiu-Wai its source is clear enough: his performance in *Lust, Caution*, his only 2007 release. 'Charismatic' is a generous or charitable enough term for Leung's acting in *Lust, Caution*, in which he plays a Shanghai official who collaborates with the occupying Japanese Army during the Second Sino-Japanese War, and whose duties involve exposing Chinese nationalists and consigning them to death. As the film earned notoriety for its reasonably graphic sex scenes, it offers a useful case through which to see how films present him as a sexual being, and on what performance resources he draws in his characterisation of the official, Mr Yee.[4]

*Lust, Caution* features five scenes of characters having sex.[5] All involve actress Tang Wei's character, Wong Chia Chi, who goes undercover as Mak Tai Tai in a plot to assassinate Yee. Before seducing Yee, Wong must first unburden herself of her virginity and practise having sex, which she does in two scenes of semi-awkward coupling with a comrade-in-arms, Liang Jun Sheng (Ko Yu-Luen, aka Lawrence Ko). In the film's second half, Wong, now known as Mak, has sex three times with Yee. Each of these scenes is about two and a half minutes long, including what passes for foreplay. Yee and Mak's first sexual encounter is a de facto rape, with

Yee assaulting Mak by throwing her against a wall, tearing at her underwear, beating her with a belt and binding her hands before rough rear-entry coupling. Both remain mostly clothed for the scene, set in daytime. Leung is silent until the end of the scene, when he tosses her coat to her and leaves the bedroom. His actions are aggressive throughout, with sudden movements and an angry expression on his face. He appears in a range of shot types, though many close-ups show his face turned away from the camera or obscure it behind his or Tang's hair. The scene demonstrates Yee's dominance of Mak, though its last shot is a close-up of her face breaking into a sly smile, as her goal had been to arouse his desire and thus to facilitate his later entrapment.

Yee and Mak's second sex scene also occurs in daytime, though now with both characters naked. Yee does not speak, and Mak is mostly silent, but as they lie curled together near the end of the scene, she bluntly declares, 'give me an apartment', again asserting her command of the situation, this time not just to viewers but to Yee. Leung's gestures and body language soften over the course of the scene. Initially he puts his hand on her throat, appearing to choke her, but his touch becomes less violent and

Leung's mature, sculpted body on display in *Lust, Caution* (2007)

more tender as they continue, and by the end the pair embrace, in what could read as romantic intimacy. (Still, while the scene includes licking and kissing, Yee and Mak do not kiss on the lips.) The scene's lighting approximates daytime interior sunlight, this time with warmer tones than in the first sex scene, the violent rape, which shows rain falling outside to motivate its cold lighting (and which put characters in clothing to match, both in blues shading toward grey). While many shots emphasise a tangle of body parts seen in fragments, Leung's face often appears in close-ups, his expressive eyes on display. While his emotions and mindset remain ambiguous, the scene's final shots of him reveal a look of apparent concern, even regret, on his face. The few scenes of Yee in his work role present him as an understated villain, dispassionately overseeing imprisonments and executions. In the wake of his lusty encounters with Mak, intimate close-ups allow him to register emotions legible as humane, if not as outright sympathetic.

Notably, all three scenes include some rear-entry sex, indicating Yee's aggression, his unromantic temperament and his ostensible degradation of Mak (given rear-entry and anal sex's connotations, valid or not, of male power over women).

Intimate close-ups in *Lust, Caution* allow Leung a degree of expressivity

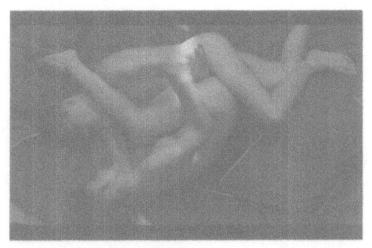

*Lust, Caution's* sex scenes keep Leung's genitals out of view

The conceit also lends the scenes the frisson of sex acts beyond the standard missionary position, and most practically of course, conveniently shields Leung's genitals. The scenes' power dynamics, and the overall narrative situation – assassination plotter seduces traitorous, murderous bureaucrat – challenge any viewer efforts to read the scenes as expressly pleasurable. These conditions also restrict Leung from acting in a charming manner, if not in a charismatic one.

For the third scene, a nighttime setting engenders still warmer lighting, and much of the frame appears in deep shadow throughout. Mak now assumes the dominant role in the unspoken power dynamic, even placing a pillow over Yee's eyes and staring at his holstered gun hanging near the bed. Yee yanks the pillow from his face in a gesture of panic or victimhood, and in his few close-ups he appears a desperate or fearful figure, seemingly anticipating his demise. More than in the previous sex scene, shots and body positions obscure his features, rendering him a servicer of Mak, an anonymous if visually appealing mass of slick, black hair and taut, smooth skin. While both scenes featuring nudity supply fuller views of actress Tang, Leung's lean but muscular frame also receives

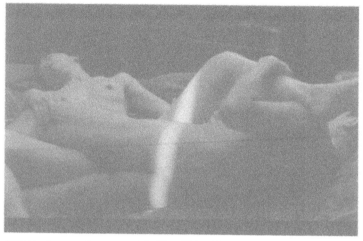

Naked bodies as performance tools for Tang Wei and Leung in *Lust, Caution*

considerable visual attention. Though bare backs and bottoms may not routinely be understood as performance tools in dramatic cinema, in *Lust, Caution* they account substantially for Leung's sex appeal, particularly when the film limits views of his face and when his character cannot be played as a genial, charming one.

Let me interrupt the reading of Leung's performance to introduce a further critical context. The recognition of a given screen role as charismatic or sexy depends upon a range of performance signs as well as on viewers' responses to those signs, and their acceptance of, or at least familiarity with, surrounding social protocols. Or, as Cynthia Baron and Sharon Marie Carnicke argue, 'interpretations of filmic gestures are influenced by viewers' personal associations with comparable social gestures and their acquaintance with the gestural conventions of pertinent aesthetic traditions' (2008: 4). Beyond performance, elements of *mise-en-scène*, lighting and framing, along with sound and editing choices, help determine the presentation and appeal of a given actor's work. Foregrounding acting in this dynamic system, Baron and Carnicke observe further that 'performance details extend, support, and counterbalance impressions, meaning, and significance created by other filmic choices' (2008: 5). Lest we forget too, other performers contribute as well, as apparent in regular, subjective judgments of paired or ensemble performers' on-screen 'chemistry'. In this regard, I offer a final point from Baron and Carnicke: 'actors adjust the quality and energy of their gestures, voices, and actions to fit their characters' shifting desires *and interactions with others*' (2008: 44, my emphasis). In total, screen charisma involves individual performance tools, interpersonal dynamics on screen, scene space and cinematographic attributes, and viewers' situation of all these within personal and socially constructed landscapes of meaning.

We might re-read *Lust, Caution*'s sex scenes in terms of this array of criteria, but for a less intense expression of Leung's sexual charisma, we can turn instead to earlier roles that make different demands on him and on viewers. Such roles show Leung delivering charismatic, engaging performances even when in narrative situations that lack the cultural and ideological weight of, say, occupied Shanghai. I offer in this regard a brief scene from 1993's *Tom, Dick and Hairy*, an ensemble comedy targeting the local Hong Kong audience, not the international art-cinema market central to *Lust, Caution*'s critical reputation or the regional East Asian markets where it earned its greatest receipts.[6] In the comedy, Leung plays title character Tom, one of a trio of bachelors sharing an apartment and involved in overlapping sexual misadventures. He first appears as an unhappy husband-to-be, his fiancée, Joyce (Jay Lau Kam-ling), fulfilling her sexual needs but not his. Tom soon meets a free-spirited bar hostess, Cat (Ann Bridgewater) – basically a prostitute, though the film does not dwell on this status – and spends a sex-drenched night, and day, with her. The film, a sex farce, refers repeatedly to orgasms and sex organs, even requiring its three leads to play fantasy scenes as their own penises, wearing skullcaps and form-fitting white jumpsuits. Despite this bawdiness, the film includes no nudity, and shots of Leung in the sex scenes reveal only his bare chest and legs. Instead, his appeal is presented through facial expressions, including boyish grins

A bare-chested, ingratiating Leung with Ann Bridgewater in *Tom, Dick and Hairy* (1993)

and solicitous gazes, as well as looks of glum dejection when both Joyce and Cat spurn his affections in different ways. Evidencing the chemistry necessary for his character's on-screen appeal, Leung's Tom repeatedly makes eye contact with and virtually beams at his paramour Cat, quickly abandoning a cool posture in favour of a self-presentation akin to that of a smitten adolescent.

The following year, Leung co-starred in what remains of his better-known films in global circulation, director Wong Kar-Wai's *Chungking Express*. Leung here plays a low-key beat policeman, who we first meet as the boyfriend of an airline stewardess, and who then becomes the object of an eccentric food-counter worker's romantic infatuation. After a scene of him in uniform, the film takes us to his small apartment for a languorous sexual episode with his stewardess girlfriend. Leung's unnamed character (he is only 'Officer 663') retains the boyishness of *Tom, Dick and Hairy*'s protagonist as he wrestles playfully with Valerie Chow's also-unnamed stewardess. The scene concludes with him in repose, lying in white briefs and tank top next to his sweat-flecked girlfriend. His character wears the same outfit in later scenes as he mopes around his apartment following her apparent exit from

Leung relaxes after a romp with his stewardess girlfriend Valerie Chow in *Chungking Express* (1994)

the relationship. The romance scene shows Leung as physically attractive but not dominant, as smiling or quietly contented, and as individually charismatic but also mindful of his companion: he smokes a cigarette and moves a toy plane through the air with studied indifference (gazing low and out of frame) before piloting it toward the woman and turning his attention to her.

The emphasis in films such as *Lust, Caution* on Leung's and his female co-stars' unclothed bodily display suggests a subsidiary dimension of what Yiman Wang (2015: 173) terms 'epidermo-centric' constructions of identity. However, the 1990s Hong Kong releases I gloss here play mostly to local audiences, with some theatrical and home-video circulation more widely in the East Asian region.[7] Similarly, as noted, *Lust, Caution* in particular attracts audiences in far greater numbers within East Asia than elsewhere. Thus, while texts such as *Chungking Express* and *Lust, Caution* indeed circulate internationally, Leung's and co-stars' displays do not function principally as exotic representations of foreign others, but as more or less racy iterations of already familiar stars' personas and acting talents.

Nonetheless too, as both Kwai-Cheung Lo and Man-Fung Yip remind us, local Hong Kong cinema occupies 'a chronic state of in-betweenness', developing its own expressive tradition but also transculturally borrowing elements from Hollywood, Chinese and other cinemas and popular cultures: a cosmopolitan territory's cosmopolitan cinema (Yip 2015: 94; referencing Lo 2005: 108–114).[8] *Lust, Caution* is also a thoroughly transnational, hybrid production, involving mainland Chinese, Taiwanese, Hong Kong and US financing, locations and personnel.[9] Both Hong Kong films and transnational co-productions position the cosmopolitan Leung at the centre of filmic traditions that unself-consciously represent Chinese subjects – sometimes literally unadorned ones – while also linking to ostensibly Western or Westernised codes of epidermo-centrism and ocularcentricity.

These brief scenes, I hope, partly demonstrate Leung's cosmopolitan screen image. The loose-fitting suits he wears in his 1980s and 1990s Hong Kong films with contemporary settings (excluding his many historical martial-arts roles or those in Wong Kar-Wai's period films with 1960s settings) anchor him in particular style contexts. Other filming and acting choices – his intermittent shirtlessness or nudity, camera attention to his face and his consistent use of silence as an acting tool – make him legible across spaces and times, culturally situated but also mobile. And of course, despite the warm climate of the Hong Kong settings in which many of Leung's characters operate, he and co-stars do keep their clothes on most of the time. In many cases, films restrict bodily display to shots of characters in practical warm-weather outfits. For example, after dining with a date in 2001s *Fighting for Love*, Leung's character, Tung-choi, walks outdoors with her, removing his sport jacket to reveal a sleeveless dress shirt beneath. At last viewers see the 'sex in a white suit' Leung represents for *Giant Robot* contributor Claudine Ko. In the scene, we can also note Leung's ingratiating, minimally demonstrative body language as he tries to appeal romantically to the prickly Siu-tong (Sammi Cheng). Here Leung constructs appeal not through forceful

'Sex in a white suit': Leung and Sammi Cheng in *Fighting for Love* (2001)

actions or strong physicality, but through his performance of ease and of attentiveness to his co-star Cheng.

## Modelling performative display

Leung's work and stardom throw many categories into relief: performance across (and beyond) genres, codes of screen masculinity and race, professional relationships with popular as well as designated auteur directors, and the varying star personas and reception discourse that arise in local, regional and international contexts. While I have not addressed viewing or spectatorship across racial and ethnic categories, or reception overall, the films I investigate above reach their largest audiences within East Asia, so Leung performs principally for East Asian viewers' consumption. At the same time, he stands as a cosmopolitan performer who has worked and earned accolades in multiple regional and global contexts. As noted too, Hong Kong and its cinema, as points of cultural intersection and hybridity, both exemplify global cosmopolitanism. Leung's charismatic performances and eye-catching physical displays thus provide indices for wider understandings of the shaping and manifestation of male sex appeal in contemporary screen production. To understand Leung's charismatic performance in wider contexts, we should also address constructions of race, gender and the body in Hong Kong, China and beyond.

While necessarily mediated, film stardom is also a material phenomenon, relying on the visual (and sometimes audible) evidence of screen performance. That performance puts the actor's physical form on display, with cinematic convention tending to emphasise the face and body. Because Leung is a Chinese male whose performances travel into contexts in which he appears a member of either a majority or minority race, theorisations of Chinese masculinity and the male body can suggest the terms on which his work circulates in screen culture. Similarly, because many of Leung's films (and his television work as well) call on his good looks and sexual and romantic charisma for narrative and aesthetic purposes, this study can benefit too from theorisations of male sexuality and sex appeal, particularly as those function in media texts.

Leung is best known internationally for his work in films – seven to date, from *Days of Being Wild* (1990) to *The Grandmaster* – from Hong Kong director Wong Kar-Wai. In his monograph on the filmmaker, Gary Bettinson argues that Wong's films offer 'an aesthetic of disturbance': 'an aesthetic that roughens existing norms in ways that both nourish and nonplus the eye, posing obstacles to the viewer's perception and understanding' (2015: 24). Such an aesthetic presents challenges for actors as well, not only with recurring production delays impeding discrete performances but also with elliptical narration, ambiguous causality and characterisation, and strongly aestheticised cinematography and *mise-en-scène* threatening to decentralise character and performance. Nonetheless, Bettinson's book title, *The Sensuous Cinema of Wong Kar-Wai*, identifies the possible sensory, and implicitly physical, appeals of Wong's films. The sensuous landscapes of Wong's films give Leung space to engage richly with viewers' senses, in ways that may bridge the divide between sensuousness (activating the sensory faculties) and sensuality (arousing viewers' sexual desires). In Wong's films and others, the way a given performance registers as romantically or sexually appealing depends on its situation in narrative and cinematic space. As such, while throughout this work I account for the details of Leung's performances in isolation, I frame them too in the contexts of given screen texts and Leung's overall television and film activity.

In the remainder of this chapter, I examine portions of Leung's performances in *Days of Being Wild* and *Happy Together* (1997), alongside critical models of physical display on screen, particularly display of the naked or semi-naked male body. I bring together theorisations of male display attentive to Western contexts as well as specifically Asian ones. As his star image depends strongly on perceived sex appeal, this book's overall study of Leung requires a model of cinematic sexual display that accounts for the conditions of East Asian cultural production as well as the international circulation of screen representations. As such, the following sections probe the conditions and limits of Asian male visibility in commercial screen contexts.

## Sexy acting and acting out sex in *Days of Being Wild* and *Happy Together*

A brief glossing of two scenes from Leung's 1990s films indicates some of the dimensions of sexually charismatic screen performance. Consider first his star-worthy cameo in Wong's *Days of Being Wild*. Leung appears only in the film's final scene, initiating a storyline ostensibly planned for a longer version of the film but never completed.[10] Following separate scenes of the film's principals – Leslie Cheung and Andy Lau on a train, Carina Lau arriving in the Philippines, then Maggie Cheung at work alone at a ticket window – the film turns without explanation to a single-shot scene of Leung in a low-ceilinged bedroom as he finishes grooming for a night out. While Xavier Cugat's 'Jungle Drums' plays on the soundtrack, Leung meticulously files his nails, rises from sitting on a bed, puts on a sport coat and adjusts his cuffs, and moves to a table to assemble what appear to be a gambler's tools, including a large wad of bills and decks of cards. He also places a variety of items in each of his many pockets (coat, vest and trousers), including two packs of cigarettes, a set of keys, a number of coins he picks up one by one, and finally a pocket kerchief he carefully folds. He combs his gelled hair and studies his appearance in a cloudy mirror, moves back toward the bed to unplug three separate lights, then finally tosses out the window the cigarette he has managed to keep in his mouth for the duration of the scene. The close camera position and lack of editing emphasise Leung as the scene's focus, as does the slight camera movement that keeps him in the frame (sometimes matched with his blurry mirror image) after he steps momentarily outside of camera view. Leung's loose-fitting suit carries meaning as well, beyond further expressing the film's early 1960s milieu and joining the actor's own movements to the tight bedroom space. In her work on costuming, Stella Bruzzi observes that 'Men's dress is usually considered to be innately stable and to lack the "natural tendency to change" of women's clothes, ... being functional rather than decorative' (1997: 68). In the scene, Leung's outfit is both functional and decorative – functional in his placement of ostensible gambler's tools in nearly all his available pockets, and decorative as underscored by his careful performance of dressing up, including aligning his cuffs and folding the handkerchief (itself possibly pure decoration, though functional if intended, for example, for sleight of hand).

The scene's lack of explicit integration into the film's storyline consolidates Leung's status here as an enigmatic figure. The film's main plot concludes just previously, with the ladies' man played by Leslie Cheung sitting immobile on a train, the victim of a gunshot. The coda with Leung, then, implicitly marks

Leung spruces up in tight quarters at the end of *Days of Being Wild* (1990)

him as a replacement lady-killer, though not one who actually interacts with any other characters.[11] (Though not named in the film, credits identify the character as Chow Mo-Wan, who Leung will play again, in very different forms but with romance on the menu for each, in *In the Mood for Love* and *2046*.) Leung's isolated preparation, in a tightly contained space, for apparent social activity suggests instead endless potential narratives of romantic possibility. In the low-ceilinged room – seemingly a cramped basement apartment – he also manages to appear sexy and composed despite never being able to stand erect. The lens choice, close camera position and indirect lighting sources create subtle distortions, lending depth to the confined space. The oblong position of the clouded mirror further complicates spatial relations, though offering a focal point for Leung's gaze and occasionally reflecting a portion of his face and chest. Overall, Leung constructs a charismatic performance amid a highly stylised visual field, in a space that limits natural stances and motions.

Leung is not so elusive a presence in *Happy Together*, where his is the first face seen on screen (in a passport photo in the opening shots, intercut with the film's titles). *Happy Together* pairs

Leung with Leslie Cheung in a romantic (or in many respects, post-romantic) relationship that plays out mostly in Buenos Aires before concluding in Taipei. Following the brisk credit sequence, the first extended scene, and most of the next twenty-plus minutes of the film, is in grainy black and white. This chromatic choice, along with the sparsely decorated bedroom setting, brief shot durations, intermittent handheld camerawork and blurred images, powerfully contrasts with *Days of Being Wild*'s aesthetic (as well as the colour values of Wong's intervening three features). Even more notably, as for many scenes in the film, Leung appears here only in white briefs, first leaning against a tarnished, full-length mirror, before lustily grappling with Cheung in the film's one semi-explicit sex scene.[12] The men kiss aggressively, straining the springs on a twin bed. Cheung straddles Leung, then flips over as the camera moves in for a tight two-shot while the two men simulate anal sex (Leung pitching, Cheung catching). Throughout the scene, blocking and camera position emphasise Leung's face rather than Cheung's. Leung's expressions are mostly serious, showing concentration if not obvious passion until penetration begins, by which point both he and Cheung appear with teeth clenched and eyes tightly shut. The scene does not obey the conventions Susan Bordo ascribes to cinematic sex scenes. In mainstream film (implicitly Hollywood's), Bordo writes, 'The male's participation is largely represented by caressing hands, humping buttocks and – on rare occasions – a facial expression of intense concentration' (2000: 191). As in *Days of Being Wild*, Leung's face is on display for most of the two-minute scene, but his nearly naked body also serves as a key performance tool, in what would be his most graphic sex scene until *Lust, Caution* ten years later.

Leung reportedly found the scene demanding, if partly as a result of director Wong's changing plans. Cinematographer Christopher Doyle recounts that 'Tony is devastated when it's all done. "Wong said all I had to do was kiss Leslie … . Now look how far he's pushed me"' (Doyle 1998: 163). Leung elsewhere claims he found the role challenging in general: 'I'm not gay,

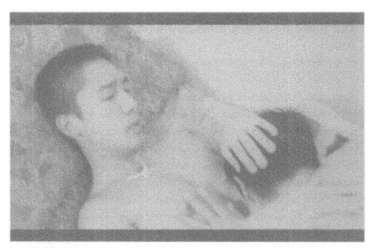

'Now look how far he's pushed me': Leung in bed with Leslie Cheung in *Happy Together* (1997)

so it was hard to get into that character. I have to find a way to get into that so I treat him as a girl, don't treat him as a man' (Wong and Nakamura 2001). Viewers might ignore the confusing explanation of how this female-identified character would occupy the penetrator role in anal sex.[13] We may wonder instead whether Leung's performance registers the ambivalence of his character, Lai Yiu-Fai, or the difficulty the actor felt in the perhaps unfamiliar terrain of the gay sex scene.[14] Since viewers learn that Lai's relationship with Cheung's character, Ho Po-Wing, is faltering, we could reasonably ascribe the shifting emotional range to Lai's own hesitancy. The film does anchor the scene in Lai's subjectivity. After Ho's opening line of dialogue – 'Lai Yiu-Fai, let's start over' – Lai's voice-over embellishes the scene and continues across the film, though not during moments such as the penetrative portion of the sex scene. As my particular focus here is Leung's use of the body, I turn next to cultural and critical frameworks to understand the source and possible reception of his physical acting.

# The male body in China and worldwide

As we investigate Leung's use of performance tools, we should recognise the specific if unstable cultural codes surrounding gender and comportment in Greater China and beyond. While such codes do not inextricably bind actors, they do indicate the degree to which particular behaviours can be received as desirable. In addition to contributing strongly to reception, constructions of idealised and normative gender roles inform, consciously or not, actors' own performance choices.

Masculinity is part of shifting and contested discourses in screen media as elsewhere in culture. Scholars of masculinity periodically default to a dominant Western notion of masculinity that overwhelmingly emphasises physical strength at the expense of speech or intellect. Kam Louie and Louise Edwards argue that, in contrast to Western constructions of masculine physicality:

The application of the contemporary Western notion of this 'macho man', whose power is made manifest in brute physical strength and unerring silence, to the Chinese case is largely inappropriate, because while there is a macho tradition in China it is not the predominant one. ... In China, the cerebral male model dominates that of the macho, brawny male. (1994: 138)

Louie and Edwards frame Chinese masculinity in terms of a dynamic opposition between literary/cerebral and martial/physical characteristics, or between *wen* and *wu*. The international circulation of films featuring East Asian stars has arguably created a flexible reception climate, in which viewers judge performers according to hybrid cultural codes rather than purely in relation (and usually subordination) to US or Western norms. In subsequent work, Louie observes that 'Chinese notions of the martial half of *wenwu* masculinity have evolved in dynamic interaction with Western (Hollywood) constructions of masculinity' (2002: 141). At the same time, he notes that the principal screen ambassadors for Chinese manhood have been action stars – Bruce Lee in the 1970s, and Jackie Chan and Chow Yun-Fat in the 1990s and beyond (although Chow's many dramatic roles have not been widely circulated) – hence the subtitle of 'Internationalising *Wu* Masculinity' in his book chapter on the phenomenon. In their original treatment of the subject, Louie and Edwards argue too that in mainland China as of the early 1990s, 'the *wu* ideal has achieved increased prominence through the Communist leadership's bid to promote the peasant or working class "hero" and … by images of masculinity from the West' (1994: 147). Still, even in roles as policemen or martial artists – from Hong Kong television's *Police Cadet* series (1984, 1985, 1988) to mainland film co-productions such as *Hero*, *Red Cliff* and *The Grandmaster* – Leung's characters balance *wen* and *wu* attributes, never privileging physical over intellectual abilities. Even as a gangland enforcer in 1995's *Cyclo*, for example, Leung's character is also, and principally, a poet (though his near-silence in that role does intersect with idealised Western masculinity's taciturnity).

Leung's work of course travels to reception contexts in which he can appear feminised, exotic or otherwise mis- or reinterpreted. As a performer, though, he has worked only in East and Southeast Asian films, shot within Asia (the one exception so far being the Argentinian locations of *Happy Together*). In his film and television works as well, he plays almost exclusively alongside other Asian performers, not in mixed East/West company as Lee, Chan and Chow have repeatedly done. Production context, location filming and co-casting thus encourage Leung to embody a Hong Kong or Chinese masculinity rather than a more profusely hybridised one, but also not to bow to essentialist constructions of Chineseness for easy legibility in global reception.

Thanks to their production context, narrative strategies and primarily intra-Asian circulation, Leung's films also largely escape the racist codings surrounding Asianness that have long informed Hollywood film and wider popular culture, particularly that of North America and Europe. Textually, Leung's films do not rely on so-called 'yellow peril' tropes, and they eschew the polarised representation of Asian men 'either as rapists or asexual eunuch figures' that Gina Marchetti (1993: 2; following Eugene Franklin Wong [1978]) identifies in decades of Hollywood interracial romances. Even if encountered through an exoticising lens or regarded as an embodiment of a stereotypical Chineseness, as a screen actor Leung communicates to viewers through his mediated body and voice. Here we might affirm Rey Chow's framing of stereotypes (building on Fredric Jameson's work) not as inherently damaging but as 'relations conducted around exteriors' (2002: 57), with such surface relations potentially presaging interior engagements as well. In other contexts involving more recent popular culture, Kwai-Cheung Lo highlights both the 'generally feminized Chinese male bodies in the Western media' (2005: 80) and Hong Kong's exported muscularity since the 1970s, noting in the latter respect that 'Hong Kong popular culture has become famous for its export of muscular Chinese bodies – from Bruce Lee, through the kung fu comics, to Jackie Chan' (2005: 81). Neither a figure of Western media nor exported as an icon of physical strength, Leung operates at a remove from these recurring tropes. Such constructions may influence reception, particularly outside East Asia. Still, even when Leung does play sexual aggressors, or contrastingly, feminised or asexual figures, he does so in the company of other East and Southeast Asians, inhibiting the formation of race- (if not gender-) based power hierarchies.

Numerous conditions, then, enable Leung to portray romantically, sexually and all-around appealing characters who operate in a Chinese, or wider East and Southeast Asian, context. In subsequent chapters I study Leung's multiple roles as cads or outright villains, from womanising rice-factory scion in *Love Unto Waste* (1986) and flirty writer Chow Mo-Wan in *2046* to double murderer in *Confession of Pain* (2006) and Japanese collaborator in *Lust, Caution*. Even these figures, though, appear as objects of desire in narrative terms and in at least some reception. Leung's work in Wong Kar-Wai's films, in which emotion typically trumps physicality, helps associate his star persona with romance, particularly as Wong's films circulate more widely internationally than do Leung's many kung fu and other action movies.[15] Reading the bodies in two of Wong's films he discusses as action films (1994's *Ashes of Time* and 1995's *Fallen Angels*), Lo argues that 'While the traditional action genre stresses the hero's masculinity and physical invulnerability, Wong's movies empty out the bodies and fill them with excess emotional drives' (2005: 100). Bypassing the question of whether these films (the former co-starring Leung) fit generic criteria for action, we can use the notion of emotional excess to help conceptualise bodily performance in films such as *Happy Together* as well.

Again, while distant in many ways from codes surrounding Hollywood and other Western cinemas, Leung does join the group of Asian men who in Hollywood representation have appeared as sexual beings, in comportment if not in representation through sex scenes and the like. In her analysis of *Year of the Dragon* (1985), Marchetti remarks on the presentation of John Lone, whose character 'functions as an object of sexual contemplation' (1993: 211) thanks to shots of his refined clothing, his practised motions, and his face and (clothed) body generally. Leung's brief appearance at the end of *Days of Being Wild* shows similar ways films may present Chinese men as sexual objects not through explicit sexual display but through clothing, gestures and overall use of actors' bodies and faces. Curiously, director Wong asserted in 1995 that Leung 'like many Hong Kong actors with television experience … was wonderfully expressive with his face but did not quite know how to utilize his body' (Siegel 2001: 189; citing Reynaud 1995: 38). For *Days of Being Wild*, Wong apparently filmed more than thirty takes of a longer scene featuring Leung (never used in the finished work) and 'finally managed to instill in Leung the necessity of concentrating on the most intimate bodily gestures' (Siegel 2001: 189). This exhaustive effort during production may account for the extant short scene's impression of Leung's gestures as stylised and studied rather than natural and casual.

Though scholars have not extensively investigated Chinese film actors as sexual or romantic icons, Kam Louie does touch on sex appeal in his analysis of Leung's near-contemporary Chow Yun-Fat, who he claims 'Chinese and Western audiences accept … as a sexy male icon' (2002: 159), based on the actor's 1980s and 1990s roles.[16] In Louie's analysis, this appeal emerges not only from Chow's looks, body language and world-weary mien but also from narratives granting his characters a sensitive, romantic outlook, as with his protagonist in the US release *The Corrupter* (1999), a '*wu* hero [who] can be a sensitive soul' (2002: 157). While Leung also plays many roles that incorporate *wu* qualities, he more emphatically embodies the *wenren* (a cultured man), a figure romantically interested in – and avowedly appealing to – women. As Louie observes, 'For there to be sexual attraction, the men should really be *wen*' (2002: 158). Better still, perhaps, that the man be Leung himself.

Beyond Louie and Edwards's theorisations of Chinese masculinity in terms of *wen–wu* interplay, scholars have probed the shifting discourses surrounding Chinese bodies in culture and representation.[17] With his career origins in Hong Kong television and film and with local Hong Kong productions dominating his résumé, Leung operates in a space of hybridised gender and representational codes. Hong Kong's longtime status as a British colony has encouraged cultural cross-pollination. By the 1960s, 'the image of the Hong Kong body was designed to fit the modern western mode of health, posture and physique' (Lo 2005: 83; paraphrasing Turner 1995). In China more broadly, John Hay claims of visual art that 'To the Western eye Chinese art has often seemed almost empty of the sexual charge that has activated so much Western art' (1994: 45). Building on Hay's work, Chris Berry notes a fundamental 'absence of the revealed body in Chinese fine art prior to contact with the west' (2006: 224), and further that 'the very concept of the "muscle" did not exist until appropriated from western anatomy studies in the nineteenth century' (2006: 224; citing Heinrich 2008). In mainland Chinese cinema, continues Berry, 'the fit body as a mark of modernization has a long history', dating back to at least the mid-1930s though 'confined to healthy and active physical participation in nation building' after the 1949 Communist takeover (2006: 226). However, by the turn of the twenty-first century, in Kam Louie's view:

As globalization progresses and Chinese men interact with the outside world more closely and intensely, the racial and cultural reference points of *wen–wu* are also rapidly changing.... The western masculine ideals represented in many of the American images are becoming more and more commonly accepted in China. (2002: 13)

Kwai-Cheung Lo articulates a similar position, noting on one hand that 'the discursive formation of Chineseness within the U.S. media remains an object of cultural and racial fantasy' (2005: 147). At the same time, he argues, 'because the Asian role is not fixed within the dominant racial discourse, Hong Kong film people can move between one culture and another, thereby increasing their agency by refashioning the transnational code of their identity' (2005: 133). Given the ongoing reconstruction of Chinese masculinity, Leung and other screen figures' gendered activity thwarts analysis strictly in terms of an essential Chineseness.

As in East Asia, cultures in the West have cycled through a range of prevailing attitudes toward both athletic and erotic bodily display of men and women, with moralising forces periodically reining in perceived excesses or vulgarities. Leung's screen representation since the 1980s partakes of cultural traditions from mainland China, a heterogeneous Hong Kong, and the West and its other satellites. His screen work has involved only Chinese and Vietnamese directors, though often alongside non-Asian cinematographers such as the Australian-born Chris Doyle (for most of Wong's films and for *Hero*) and Mexico's Rodrigo Prieto (for *Lust, Caution*). Even before circulating within and outside Asia, then, images of Leung are products of multiple sensibilities, each approaching the gendered body in complex ways.

Entertainment discourses construct Leung as a sexually, romantically or otherwise appealing figure; as a talented professional; as a regional and diasporic celebrity; and as a representative of Hong Kong and China in the era of globalisation. In later chapters I investigate his acting in a range of genres and modes in Hong Kong, Chinese and co-produced East and Southeast Asian cinema. Leung's breadth of screen performances shows the elasticity of his acting as well as different filmmakers' emphasis on some of his various abilities – at light comic performance, at gymnastic action, at static, interiorised drama and more. In all, Leung uses his body, face and voice to serve films' (and television series') narrative and generic requirements, to articulate characters of varying complexity, and to engage viewers within and beyond Asia.

# 2 1980s HONG KONG TELEVISION AND EARLY FILM EFFORTS

Chinese global stars such as Chow Yun-Fat, Maggie Cheung and Stephen Chow have earned acclaim based on their roles in internationally distributed genre films and art cinema. These and other stars, however, gained local visibility at the outset of their careers with starring roles in ensemble dramas on Hong Kong's TVB television channel. This chapter investigates Leung's 1980s television roles, his parallel work in local and regional cinema, and his simultaneous music career. Like many popular Hong Kong film actors, Leung achieved early career recognition through roles in a series of long-running TVB dramas. As one of the so-called 'Five Tigers', he co-starred in TVB efforts including the action-comedy-drama *Police Cadet* (1984) and its 1985 and 1988 sequels, and the *wuxia* dramas *The Duke of Mount Deer* (1984) and *The New Heaven Sword and Dragon Sabre* (1986).[1] Leung uses his TVB training to move into roles in Hong Kong's popular cinema, in films such as the comedies *Happy-Go-Lucky* (1987) and *I Love Maria* (1988). At the same time, he expands his repertoire with notable performances in art- or pop-art cinema works such as *Love Unto Waste* (1986, aka *Love Unto Wastes*); *A City of Sadness* (1989), his first film to earn extensive international festival exhibition; and *Days of Being Wild*, another film with a substantial international festival footprint, in which, at the end of a story featuring many of his TVB peers, Leung earns the memorable final-scene cameo discussed in Chapter 1. Overall, because of television and music's centrality to Hong Kong's broader star economy, I argue for attention to screen stars' early careers and cross-media efforts to understand their performance histories and long-term creative trajectories. Requiring him to work gruelling hours on multiple series and features each year from the mid-1980s to the early 1990s, Leung's TV and early film roles attest to his stamina. In its circulation (particularly via VCD and other home-video formats) across the global Chinese diaspora, this work indicates the initial mobility of his stardom as well.

## A rising tiger on TVB

Leung was, as noted, born in Hong Kong in 1962, and after completing secondary education early, at age fifteen, he worked a series of jobs before joining TVB's training academy in 1981. During his training, he played small roles in multiple TVB series, as well as co-starring in the short-run *Manager & Messenger* (aka *Manager and Office Boy*, 1981 or 1982). Memorably too for many Hong Kongers, in 1982 TVB made Leung a host of the children's variety show *430 Space Shuttle* (1982–1989), a role later filled by, among others, Stephen Chow and Ekin Cheng.[2] During training Leung appeared as well in his first TVB drama as a co-starring lead, the thirty-episode *Soldier of Fortune* – despite its title, a historical romance and not a war or action series – which aired in late 1982.[3] (TVB's 1980s series in their initial Hong Kong broadcasts aired each weeknight, five nights a week for six or eight weeks.) Across the 1980s Leung appeared in more than two dozen TVB series, occasionally in supporting roles but usually as the lead or second-billed actor. In the twenty-episode *The Superpower* (1983), for example, he plays the second lead role, as a contemporary Hong Konger who befriends a travelling extraterrestrial (played by fellow TVB actor Chow Yun-Fat) whom he aids in romantic pursuits and who himself benefits from the alien's otherworldly powers. In the forty-episode *The Duke of*

*Mount Deer*, Leung stars as Wai Siu-Bo (aka Wai Sui-po or Wai Xiaobao), a sometimes monk-initiate caught up in court intrigue (and occasional martial-arts battles) alongside such other emerging stars as Andy Lau and Leung's future wife, Carina Lau.[4] *The Duke of Mount Deer* adapts Louis Cha's (aka Jin Yong's) serial novel *The Deer and the Cauldron*, and Leung would play starring roles in numerous other adaptations of Cha's novels in 1980s TVB series, and later in the films *The Eagle-Shooting Heroes* (1993) and *Ashes of Time*.

Two months after *The Duke of Mount Deer*'s conclusion, Leung reappeared on TVB as the star of *Police Cadet* (aka *Police Cadet '84*, with the date added retroactively after production of its sequels), playing alongside Carina Lau again, as well as Maggie Cheung, later his co-star in numerous films from director Wong Kar-Wai the international hit *Hero*. In *Police Cadet*, Leung stars as cadet and later policeman Cheung Wai Kit, in a dramatic role calling for him to navigate numerous work, familial and romantic crises. Signed to a five-year TVB contract in 1984, Leung would return for two forty-episode continuations of the series, *Police Cadet '85* (1985) and *Police Cadet '88* (1988). In the interim, he appeared on TVB in another forty-episode series, *The Rough Ride* (1985), playing a teacher who falls in love with a policewoman. In 1985 too, he co-starred in the prestige six-episode miniseries *The Yang's Saga* (aka *The Yangs' Saga*) with a large cast of TVB stars, including not only Chow and Cheung but all of Leung's fellow Five Tigers, a group of stars (including Andy Lau) who had joined TVB between 1978 and 1981.[5] While *The Duke of Mount Deer* defines him as a mischievous rogue who lacks fighting ability, in *The Yang's Saga* he plays a more skilled fighter. He would play lead roles in additional lengthy TVB series with historical martial-arts content, including the forty-episode *The New Heaven Sword and Dragon Sabre*, another Louis Cha adaptation; and the sixty-episode *The Grand Canal* (1987).[6]

Even without comprehensively cataloguing each of Leung's many 1980s television roles, we can see that he plays dramatic, romantic, comic and action parts in series classifiable as contemporary and period dramas, *wuxia* adaptations from novels and Chinese folktales, police and youth stories, and even science fiction. While Leung's breadth of television roles is impressive, even more notable is the sheer volume of his output. Especially between 1983 and 1985, he works at an exhausting pace, particularly in comparison with the practices of other regional or national television industries (such as the US's). Leung's visibility follows from his demanding work schedule, and consequently from his versatility and endurance. As he writes in an essay in the December 1983 issue of *Hong Kong Screen Idol*, 'Acting is not always so fun. Most of you have tried to work 20 hours day job, but have you tried to work 20 hours for six months straight?' ('1983–1986: HK Screen Idols Tony Leung' n.d.).[7] The remark is no hyperbole: in 1983, he had appeared in eight series on TVB and state broadcaster RTHK, including at least three twenty-episode TVB series (*The Superpower*, *Encounter with Fortune* [aka *Lucky Ghost*] and *Angels and Devils*).[8] Then in his first 1984 series, *The Clones* (aka *The Replica*), Leung played two starring roles, as the son of a scientist and as his own identical clone, with a storyline dictating that the two characters be diametric opposites, one quiet and sweet, the other boisterous and difficult.[9] Across 1984, he appears in four TVB series: the sci-fi-inflected drama *The Clones*, running for thirty episodes in January and February; *The Duke of Mount Deer*, its forty episodes airing in July and August; the romantic drama *It's a Long Way Home*, running for twenty episodes in September and October; and finally, *Police Cadet*, with forty episodes airing from late October to late December.[10] Thus, Leung in 1984 appeared as the lead actor in over sixty hours of prime-time television (ninety episodes, each lasting forty to forty-five minutes), granting great visibility to a star image bolstered by recurring cover stories in fan magazines such as *Hong Kong Screen Idol*.

Oscillation among dramatic, romantic and action roles, as well as exhausting production schedules leading to saturation appearances in multiple long-running series each year, was characteristic of TVB's approach to talent, particularly in the 1980s. Chow Yun-Fat, Andy Lau, Stephen Chow, Maggie Cheung, Carina Lau and many other past and current Hong Kong and Chinese stars also rose to prominence with multiple leading or co-starring roles in TVB series. TVB thus exemplifies the symbiotic relationship between Hong Kong's television and film industries, with TVB series long serving as a de facto junior league, training young talent often in preparation for subsequent film roles. (Hong Kong's popular music also intersects with cinema, though in different ways thanks to distinctions between screen acting and Cantopop singing.) TVB remains Hong Kong's largest terrestrial broadcaster as well as 'the largest producer of Chinese-language programs in the world' (Chan and Fung 2013: 108–9). Many future leading directors and performers worked on TVB series in its 1970s and 1980s heyday, prompting Law Kar to term TVB and like stations 'a "Shaolin Temple" … for emerging filmmakers' (2001: 40; cited also in Teo 1997: 155). TVB's output has long circulated beyond Hong Kong too. Michael Curtin argues that TVB began to look to overseas markets after the colonial government's 1984 announcement of Hong Kong's return to Chinese rule in 1997. He notes that 'the station's resolutely capitalist practices and values seemed dramatically at odds with mainland media, which at the time revolved around state radio and newspaper propaganda' (2007: 111). Still, TVB series circulated in dubbed versions on television in mainland China and across East and Southeast Asia, as well as dubbed or subtitled in subsequent VHS, VCD and DVD release. Thus, particularly through the regionally accessible form of *wuxia* genre series, Leung by the mid-1980s had gained substantial regional visibility in screen media even without any major film roles.

Beyond the sheer endurance required to perform in so many television series, Leung's TVB work demonstrates his development as a screen actor and the aesthetic and narrative surroundings afforded to him in the early and mid-1980s. While hugely exploited in the amount of work required of him, Leung also becomes the beneficiary of a system that riskily puts a young actor at the centre of successive high-profile series. In *The Duke of Mount Deer*, for example, Leung's Wai Siu-Bo character is offscreen for only a few minutes of the series' twenty-eight–hour running time. Its mostly daytime shooting and generally high-key lighting for both indoor and outdoor scenes keep Leung on unobstructed display for large portions of each episode. The series puts his exposed body on display too. Early in the series, Siu-Bo exchanges a monk's robe for a range of elaborate, brightly coloured costumes. With many scenes set in brothels, though, Siu-Bo frequently appears shirtless, either seeking or warding off the affections of many female admirers. He appears in many martial-arts scenes as well, though mostly as the comic victim of others' assaults (sometimes replaced by a stunt double, though also repeatedly tossed and flipped himself). Beyond playing a comic underdog, Leung serves as the focal point of a lengthy, complicated narrative. He also demonstrates youthful flirtatiousness across the series, laying the groundwork for what will become a robust ladies'-man persona in later series and in dozens of films. By *The Duke of Mount Deer*'s conclusion, Siu-Bo accumulates multiple wives, who squabble with him, with each other and with his adversaries over the series' run.

Though *The Duke of Mount Deer* puts Leung in many fight scenes, it does not ask viewers to regard him as a physically powerful figure but rather as a charming weakling. His next series, *Police Cadet*, calls for some physical transformation and for the reining in of his comic physicality and facial expressiveness in favour of a manlier intensity. Particularly in its first season's many training scenes, *Police Cadet* repeatedly depicts Leung and his fellow male cadets in shorts and shirtless. The men – all thin, though most with muscular legs – run on a track, do calisthenics and often appear dressing or undressing together in dormitory and locker rooms. Leung also periodically plays scenes involving physical action, such as chasing criminal suspects on foot. While he lacks a bodybuilder's physique, most of his male co-stars are equally slender and short. In this ensemble, Leung can manifest a convincingly robust physical presence. *Police Cadet*'s narratives of training and of beat police work allow Leung to exhibit his capabilities for homosocial interaction, his ability to display generally realist physical exertion (as opposed to the stagy, perspiration-free martial-arts action of the *wuxia* series) and his convincing performance of a youthful authority figure or state representative. He will draw on all these skills and attributes for many police and action roles in 1990s and 2000s films. Indeed, *Police Cadet* casts Leung alongside future film tough guys Lau Ching-Wan (as a fellow cadet in *Police Cadet '84*) and Chow Yun-Fat (in *Police Cadet '85*, as Leung's character's uncle, a mainland transplant and non-policeman), requiring him to project a masculine intensity on par with theirs. The world of *Police Cadet* is not exclusively male or work-centred, though. Female cadets join the academy in *Police Cadet '85*. Across the series too, Leung's Wai Kit character appears in domestic and family settings, allowing him to perform both a relationship with his poor, hard-working mother and a friendship and romance with his next-door neighbour, played by fellow emerging star Maggie Cheung. As with other TVB series, *Police Cadet* combines multiple characters, storylines and emotional registers. Far from being typecast, its stars must develop wide-ranging performance abilities, often moving among comedy, action, romance and psychological realism in single episodes.

Shirtless training in sultry Hong Kong in *Police Cadet '85* (1985)

Lau Ching-Wan and Leung off duty in *Police Cadet '84* (1984)

TVB series are particularly notable for the kind of acting they privilege. Leung Wing-Fai (2015: 83) observes that, with many actors learning their craft in TVB's training academy rather than in theatre or other fine-arts contexts, Hong Kong screen acting has not privileged the Strasbergian Method or other naturalist styles. She notes local awareness of 'a distinctive Hong Kong style of acting emphasising televisual aesthetics, seen especially through a reliance on facial expressions' (2015: 128), in contrast to Hollywood and other cinemas' privileging of realist psychology. In the 1980s and 1990s too, heavy cross-media commitments and rapid film production schedules meant that 'few actors had time to prepare thoroughly for each film', and with all dialogue rerecorded in post-production, 'actors did not have to worry about precise delivery of the script' (2015: 83) during shooting. Even during his TVB years, Leung Chiu-Wai's own acting arguably exceeds the surface requirements of popular Hong Kong media, whether as cause or consequence of his parallel mid- and late 1980s work in regional art cinema. And as Leung Wing-Fai also observes, TVB actor training, 'modeled on the Shaw Studio's drama school', included studies of 'acting theory' (2015: 41) alongside presentational concerns.[11] However influential his TVB training and experience, Leung's acting is legible as a hybrid of local and regional styles indebted to multiple cultural traditions.

Both within and across series, Leung alternates between presentational and representational acting, or between self-conscious performance for an implied audience and realist-styled illusionism.[12] *Wuxia* series such as *The Duke of Mount Deer* call on him to deliver showy, surface-level performances suitable to the series' pulp-novel origins and complementing his co-stars' similarly histrionic styles. In series such as *Police Cadet*, built around contemporary social and government institutions, Leung acts in a comparatively naturalist style, and even when he and co-stars move through soap-operatic family and work plots, they modulate their performances according to conventions of present-day behaviour and interaction. Some series combine contrasting tones. *The Superpower* and *The Clones*, for example, mix fantastic content and absurd situations – recall that Leung plays an alien's earthling friend in one and a clone in the other – with character roles rooted in present-day psychological realism. TVB series thus require Leung to act both in an ostensive, exaggerated style and in a psychologised style at the border of drama and melodrama. This breadth of expression suits Leung to the demands of Hong Kong screen texts, which routinely pivot between fantastic, child-friendly farce and punishing adult drama. His elastic performance style prepares him too for the varying codes of international productions and regional art cinemas. This elasticity ensures that at least part of any given Leung performance will meet global audiences' expectations for successful or appealing acting and characterisation.

## From television to film acting

Overall, TVB series show actors such as Leung navigating constraint and freedom, exploitation and star-making good fortune. Leung works under contract for long hours in modestly budgeted series that can be received as highly formulaic. At the same time, even as a TVB trainee he earns lead roles in prime-time series, and programmes across the 1980s grant him huge amounts of screen time. These series' bright lighting design and coupling of wide staging with frequent close-ups also make Leung a highly visible performer, lending emphasis to his face and eyes, features that will come to define his star persona and acting style. High-key lighting and intermittent ensemble staging also allow for semi-free movement of actors. Leung would not be afforded such luxuries later in his many films with director Wong Kar-Wai, which involve stylised compositions with what David Bordwell (2000: 285) terms 'slit-staging' (using doorways, objects or other design features to frame performers tightly) as well as substantial shadowing that obscures actors' faces or bodies. TVB series too allow Leung to use his face and voice as expressive devices (though in terms of voice, series production as noted involves dialogue recorded separately and postsynchronised, as well as other voice actors' dubbing for release outside Cantonese-language markets). TVB series thus develop the aspects of Leung's idiolect that circulate through global arthouses in the 1990s, particularly the expressive eyes and face that suit him for roles as romantic or soulful figures.[13] They also make room for the performing traits he adopts in Hong Kong genre films from the mid-1980s to early 2000s: excitable energy, exuberant physicality and an air of lightheartedness. From 1985s *Young Cops* through films such as *Seoul Raiders* twenty years later, Leung delivers dozens of smiling, ingratiating performances. Indeed, in films such as *Young Cops*, *Tokyo Raiders* and *Seoul Raiders*, Leung gives clownish performances akin to those of Jackie Chan, though with considerably less stuntwork and considerably more sexual charisma. (At the very least, Leung's characters demonstrate far deeper interest in women than Chan's do in his Hong Kong and Hollywood action-comedies.)

Many later film efforts require Leung to rein in his repertoire of acting tools. He performs as mute characters in dramatic works such as *The Lunatics* (1986) and *A City of Sadness*; for the latter, Leung allegedly asked director Hou Hsiao-Hsien to make his character deaf and mute rather than having to explain the character's inability to speak the film's main languages of Taiwanese and Japanese. In many local or part-local films he would play blind characters as well: for example, in 1996's *Blind Romance*, 2003's *Sound of Colors* and the 2012 mainland co-production *The Silent War*. TVB series allow Leung to develop acting skills in multiple registers, and as his career evolves he periodically strips away certain attributes – speaking, looking, even movement – for challengingly minimalist performances.

Leung's skill at facially expressive, nonverbal acting, sometimes in TVB roles and extensively in later film acting, helps position his work for accessible international recognition. Different roles call on Leung to be loquacious or taciturn, smiling or sombre, youthful or mature. Director preference, storytelling requirements and films' predominant spoken languages further influence the type of performance Leung will give. TVB series and later film roles also involve regular displays of physicality, with Leung using his full (and sometimes partly naked) body as a performance tool. In *Police Cadet* and in his multiple *wuxia* series, he gesticulates, runs and participates in martial-arts fights. Leung's TVB series and later films circulate widely in East and Southeast Asia and across the global Chinese diaspora, and his combination of physicality and facial expressiveness forms a core component of texts that afford him starring roles. As such, Leung represents a significant creative resource for the TVB channel and for film studios as they seek to distribute works regionally and globally in the 1980s and 1990s.

To situate their characters and stories, TV series such as *Police Cadet* and films such as *Young Cops*, *Happy-Go-Lucky* and *I Love Maria* feature contemporary settings and production design comparable to the imagery of global advertising and transnational popular culture. Cynthia Baron argues that the 1989 film *The Killer* (which does not feature Leung) 'gives cosmopolitan audiences avenues for emotional contact by framing the characters' significant encounters and experiences in color schemes and compositions one would find in glossy print ads … touching TV spots … and programs' cliffhanger scenes' (2004: 305). Hong Kong police series and films in police and crime genres use similar imagery, shooting on city streets adorned with near-ubiquitous neon signs, adding stylised, coloured lighting for nighttime and indoor scenes, and costuming many characters in trendy youth fashions. *Police Cadet* and *Young Cops* present Leung in bright, often pastel colours – in *Police Cadet*, when not in cadet or officer uniform, or in gym shorts and shirtless, Leung wears outfits such as loose white pants and a fuchsia shirt, or sleeveless, scoop-necked terry-cloth sweatshirts (in yellow, red or white) with jeans or shorts. *Young Cops* finds him in numerous new-wave preppy outfits, like a sporty white pants-and-jacket ensemble with a yellow shirt, that would fit easily into a 1980s Duran Duran video. Also in the film, a sequence leading up to his character's wedding offers a montage of high-life good times iconographically akin to luxury lifestyle advertising. By the time of his co-starring role in *Hard-Boiled*, Leung's designer-clothed character appears just as much a slave to fashion as Chow had been in the distinctively styled *The Killer*. The same year, the gangster parody *The Days of Being Dumb* (1992) puts him for many sequences in a bright-red, tailored suit and matching shirt. Earlier, in TVB's historical martial-arts series, Leung's monk's robes and his elaborate silk or satin costumes, while not part of the lexicon of 1980s global postmodernism, also register as familiar or appealing for many viewing groups, particularly in East and Southeast Asia.

Wider dynamics of screen globalisation also inform Leung's acting and stardom. His activity in 1980s TVB (and other channels') productions intersects with existing and emerging political, cultural and economic developments. Michael Curtin argues that in the 1980s, 'converging factors prodded TVB to globalize its operations' (2007: 112). These factors included the looming handover to China, declining local interest in TVB's factory-like productions and consumers' turn to other entertainment forms such as cinema, karaoke and video games.[14] Leung's roles in *wuxia* dramas locate him firmly within popular traditions in Hong Kong print and screen media. At the same time, these roles, in accessible or widely known adaptations of Louis Cha stories and other Chinese literature and folktales, formed part of TVB's export offerings to regional channels and to TVB's own video stores in cities with sizeable Chinese populations (opening in the late 1980s and 1990s, for example, in London and Vancouver).[15] Series such as *The Duke of Mount Deer, The Yang's Saga* and *The New Heaven Sword and Dragon Sabre* represented the sort of content – 'series about ancient dynasties and kung fu heroes' – with appeal for ethnic Chinese viewers as well as wider audiences in East and Southeast Asia.[16] Leung's television acting of course includes non-*wuxia* roles as well, and series such as the sci-fi/comedy/drama *The Superpower* and the long-running *Police Cadet* would also encounter minimal cultural discounts elsewhere in Asia and the Chinese diaspora, though plotlines of official corruption in *Police Cadet*'s sequels would limit its distribution in mainland China.[17] Overall, both before and amid his appearances in popular Hong Kong and other East Asian films, Leung's performances circulated extensively on television and home video not just in Hong Kong but internationally. Whether connected to TVB's success in cultivating local talent such as the Five Tigers and their peers, to the company's regional distribution efforts in the 1980s and beyond, or to other developments involving local broadcast competition and mainland Chinese and overseas markets, Leung's rise to prominence occurs amid the early stages of long-term disruptions affecting TVB and other Hong Kong screen-industry companies.

TVB producers' decision to locate Leung at the forefront of numerous long-running series, Leung's own remarkable time and labour investments in those series, and fan-magazine and other publicity surrounding his onscreen exploits and offscreen romantic life all served to make him a ubiquitous presence in Hong Kong and wider East and Southeast Asian screen culture in the 1980s and beyond. (Indeed, his starring role as Wai Siu-Bo in *The Duke of Mount Deer* proved memorable enough that he would effectively reprise it nearly a decade later in the genre-mixing film *Hero – Beyond the Boundary of Time* [1993], where his womanising princeling time-travels from the seventeenth century to the present for fantasy and comic action.) His hundreds of hours of television roles granted him visibility before and alongside his extensive film acting beginning in the mid-1980s. His heavy TVB production schedules, as well as stated uninterest in financial reward, limited his initial opportunities for film work.[18] By 1989, though, he appeared in three or more films each year, reaching his peak of productivity in 1993, when he played lead or supporting roles in up to ten films (compared to six in 1991, three in 1992 and four in 1994).[19] Despite this prolific output, Leung's reputation even during periods of heavy film work has been as a discriminating actor. Lisa Odham Stokes claims that:

Unlike many others, Leung never took part in the Hong Kong method of filming that allowed a hot star to work on several films at once (using photo doubles in every possible shot), and complete up to 20 or more films a year. He has opted instead to mix one or two long-term projects with a couple of "quickies." (2007: 265)

The long-term projects have included most famously his collaborations with director Wong Kar-Wai, in films such as *Ashes of Time* with protracted production schedules of eighteen months or longer.[20] Leung's first work with Wong coincidentally highlights other peculiarities of Hong Kong's entertainment sector. Like many of his fellow TVB alumni, Leung did not escape the Triad activity plaguing the Hong Kong film industry in the 1980s and 1990s, activity including kidnappings and extortion of producers and stars (for example, many sources name Andy Lau as a victim of Triad extortion). In 1990, criminal activity indirectly impacted Leung's career. As examined in Chapter 1, the final scene of *Days of Being Wild* features, without explanation, Leung glamorously combing his hair in front of a mirror. Some discourse around the film avows that Leung was offered a larger part but declined because of personal circumstances: his girlfriend, Carina Lau, was briefly kidnapped during the film's production.[21] The kidnapping was an attempt to pressure her, not Leung, but the event indicates some of the conditions major Hong Kong performers had to negotiate during this period.

## Leung as emerging film star

Prior to his celebrated work with Wong, Leung's early film work included lead roles in local films such as *The Lunatics*, *Happy-Go-Lucky* and *People's Hero* (1987) that allowed him to demonstrate his versatility. He began film acting with a small role in 1983s *Mad, Mad 83*, then played romantic leads in two 1985 films, the comedy *Fascinating Affairs* and the action-comedy *Young Cops*.[22] These roles largely consolidated his existing screen persona, casting him as young men with romantic and comic temperaments, if in the present day rather than amid the past settings of the *wuxia* television series. (Thus, as for TV series such as *Police Cadet*, Leung appears in these films with a full head of hair in a contemporary style rather than with the shaved head of *The Duke of Mount Deer* or the elaborately long-haired wig of *The New Heaven Sword and Dragon Sabre*.) *Young Cops*, about a trio of, yes, young cops, who pursue young women – and occasionally, criminals – plays on Leung's on- and offscreen celebrity. His character's name, Leung Sui-Po, combines his own surname with the given name of his *Duke of Mount Deer* character, fresh in many local viewers' minds from its broadcast less than a year earlier.

　　*Young Cops* also offers Leung character attributes that feature across most of his popular television and film roles. Producers usually cast him as a middle– or upper-middle–class charmer. (*The Duke of Mount Deer* makes him an orphan, though even here he acts more as a man of leisure and play than a working-class figure.) While invested in women, usually as romantic interests, Leung also tends to be part of a male duo or group. Correspondingly, given the sexual politics of 1980s Hong Kong comedies, his scenes in *Young Cops* and many other buddy films veer into mildly homophobic banter. At the same time, this banter shows him generally at ease with other men, a dynamic visible in later films as well. The buddy comedy *The Days of Being Dumb* includes a subplot in which Leung and co-star Jackie Cheung initially fail to romance a pair of women shown to viewers as lesbians, although one eventually succumbs to Leung's charms. As in other films of the period, homosexuality here appears chiefly a subject for comedy. In keeping with the tone of Hong Kong popular comedies, though, *The Days of Being Dumb* treats lesbianism and men's responses to it in a gentle rather than mean-spirited way. In addition, the film depicts Leung and Cheung as cosily intimate, appearing together in nearly every scene. At one point, seeking to become Triads, the pair strip down to give each other elaborate tattoos, then try to do some bare-chested enforcing. In another scene, Cheung curls up next to Leung in bed (a bed they share with Anita Yuen's ex-lesbian). Finally, a frame story ultimately reveals the male duo to be sharing a prison cell. Later in the 1990s, Leung would again emphasise the softer side of his persona, for gay roles in films such as *Happy Together* and the Jackie Chan farce *Gorgeous* (1999).[23] Like some *wuxia* television roles though not so much the drama *Police Cadet*, the film *Young Cops* also fits Leung into the template of the brazen womaniser who actually succeeds with women, a divide he navigates with geniality and a degree of comic self-effacement.

Leung returned to the large screen in summer 1986, appearing in two films during an uncharacteristically lengthy absence from new television series. (*Police Cadet '85* concluded in late December 1985, and *The New Heaven Sword and Dragon Sabre* began airing in November 1986, with Leung featured in opening titles but his character not introduced until partway through the series.) *The Lunatics*, the directorial debut of actor-turned-director Derek Yee Tung-Sing, represented the first major departure from Leung's affable screen persona. In a relatively rare example of a Hong Kong social-problem film, *The Lunatics* casts Leung in a bravura supporting role as Doggie, a mentally ill homeless man. (Chow Yun-Fat plays a similar but smaller role in the film.) Doggie's childlike affect and muteness may arouse viewer sympathies, but his motley dress and borderline-violent derangement enable Leung to act in a novel dramatic register. In the film's opening sequence, for example, he brandishes a meat cleaver and threatens female patrons in a large indoor market. Though Leung was not among the main protagonists, the role located him in a new milieu of critical acclaim, as *The Lunatics* won two awards (out of five total nominations) at the 1987 Hong Kong Film Awards. At those awards, Leung also earned a Best Actor nomination, for his lead role in his other 1986 film, *Love Unto Waste*, released two months after *The Lunatics*. *Love Unto Waste* was the second film from eventual festival-celebrated director Stanley Kwan and earned notice too for Chow Yun-Fat's co-starring performance as an eccentric, lonely police detective. Leung stars as the young manager of a family rice business, a character who romances numerous women. The role again calls on talents he had displayed in television work: his character has moments of dramatic intensity as well as romantic charm, and Leung's acting humanises a figure who might otherwise appear an outright cad. (In the opening scene, for example, his character celebrates his birthday at a bar with drunken singing and obnoxious behaviour around women, before vomiting on a group of bar patrons.)

Appearing in two films again the following year, Leung continues to play roles that either bring together the range of attributes he displays across TVB series or focus his efforts in an intense dramatic register. In the former category, *Happy-Go-Lucky* casts him as a repo man involved in comic, romantic, dramatic and action plots. Here he demonstrates verbal and slapstick comedy utilising body, face and voice, as well as playing scenes in a realist acting style. He also appears in multiple comic action sequences: in go-kart racing, an ice-skating fight scene, and a climactic car-racing and crash sequence. Next, in the late-1987 release *People's Hero* (also from director Derek Yee), he plays a young accomplice in a heist gone wrong, the story unfolding as a bank-hostage drama with echoes of *Dog Day Afternoon* (1975). *People's Hero* earned Leung his first major acting award, Best Supporting Actor at 1988s Hong Kong Film Awards. Returning to a comic style, in the following year's sci-fi action comedy *I Love Maria* he plays a supporting role as a blundering reporter who investigates criminal activity involving giant and humanoid robots.

Each of these films offered Leung a platform for further demonstration of skills displayed in TVB series. These include the comic temperament and mischievous but unthreatening ladies'-man demeanour he brings to *The Superpower* and *The Duke of Mount Deer*, the ability to gesticulate through action scenes in *The Duke of Mount Deer* and other *wuxia* series (in earlier series, mostly not administering but receiving kicks and punches, but nonetheless a

Leung mugs for the camera during an ice-rink skirmish in the comedy *Happy-Go-Lucky* (1987)

visible part of action scenes), the high emotions portrayed in dramas such as *Soldier of Fortune*, *The Clones* and the *Police Cadet* series, and the romantic chemistry and general likeability in evidence across his 1980s television work. With its more contained nature and typically higher production values compared to TVB series, Leung's film work also begins to shape him into a more distinctive figure: a film star known for discrete roles rather than a television star known for hypervisibility. Film will allow him to explore darker characters as well. He plays predominantly prosocial characters across his television career, but in film he begins to take periodic criminal roles, such as the reluctant bank robber of *People's Hero*, the comic Triad wannabe of *The Days of Being Dumb*, the stylish assassin (and undercover policeman) of *Hard-Boiled*, and, perhaps most alarmingly in his mid-career, the sadistic sociopath cop of *The Longest Nite* (1998). Together, film and television roles demonstrate Leung's ability to perform on both sides of legal and moral divides.

Leung's heavy exposure as a television actor, rather than typecasting him, grants him a broad portfolio of performances and prepares him and viewing communities for the many later roles that both consolidate and expand his acting persona. Recognised in Hong Kong and elsewhere thanks to the popularity of TVB series, Leung can take risks with roles such as that of the mentally ill Doggie in *The Lunatics* and the deaf-mute Wen-Ching in *A City of Sadness*. Both these films show his range to local audiences and expose him to international viewerships through festival screenings. Leung's television roles circulate widely through TVB's distribution networks and allow the rapid development of his acting and star image, prior to his recognition by the international film community. As such, the television phase of his lengthy career is instrumental in establishing his screen persona and in coupling professional training with the relative security of a long-term contract. His parallel and subsequent film acting earns him new international visibility, first in popular genre releases such as *A Chinese Ghost Story III* (1991) and *Hard-Boiled*, then in lead or co-starring roles in Wong's arthouse romances.

# Golden throats of Hong Kong

Before concluding this chapter on Leung's formative years as a
local Hong Kong star, an additional component of his transmedia
stardom deserves some attention: his parallel activity as a singer,
particularly in the 1990s. In a strategy common for Hong Kong
film and television stars, particularly those emerging in the 1980s,
Leung for years supplemented his already busy schedule with
a recording career, releasing ten albums from the mid-1980s
through the early 2000s. (His first record appeared in 1986, the
second in 1988, with at least eight more solo CD releases between
1993 and 2002, and best-of collections and reissues appearing
as recently as 2013.) His singing career markedly informs his
local and regional reputation and contributes to his status as a
wide-ranging talent, a prolific actor and entertainer thoroughly
enmeshed in Hong Kong's predominant cultural industries. While
not a major music star on the order of his contemporaries Andy
Lau[24] – with whom he shares vocals on the theme song for the
2002 hit film *Infernal Affairs* – or the late Leslie Cheung, local
Hong Kong audiences recognise him as both actor and singer.
Writing about Hong Kong pop music, Brian Hu (2006: 411) notes
that soundtrack releases for three of Leung's 2003 films – *My
Lucky Star*, *Infernal Affairs III* and *Sound of Colors* – helped cater
to continued market interest in the absence of new solo releases
from Leung after 2002. Such releases exemplify the maintenance
of stardom through continued visibility (and audibility) in Hong
Kong's crowded media marketplace. While largely retired from
recording and live-music performance after 2002, Leung revived
fan interest in his music abilities with a touted (if for its rarity rather
than virtuosity) performance in late-March 2013 as part of the
tribute concert on the tenth anniversary of Leslie Cheung's death.

Most of Leung's singing, in individual songs, full albums
and live performances, has been in the Cantopop style, i.e., the
Cantonese-language pop music that Western listeners might
equate with a saccharine lounge-jazz style. He has also forayed

into Mandopop, a Mandarin-language variation, presumably to appeal to the much larger mainland market. For example, he duets with mainland star (and film co-star) Zhou Xun on the soundtrack of 2011's *The Great Magician*. This duet gives mainland listeners one of the relatively few chances to hear Leung vocalising Mandarin himself. Mainland releases of most of his films, with some exceptions such as *Lust, Caution*, do not feature Leung's voice but dub his and other native Cantonese speakers' dialogue into Mandarin. Some of his singing, such as a version of Burt Bacharach and Hal David's 'I Say a Little Prayer', includes English lyrics as well. His singing thus offers a notable complement to his screen image, since despite English fluency (sometimes on display in interviews), none of Leung's film roles to date include English dialogue. In Cantopop and Mandopop variations, Leung's singing foregrounds the emotional expressiveness characteristic of both forms, helping define his multimedia persona in terms of romantic longing and unrestrained emotion. As Hu argues, Hong Kong's gossipy entertainment culture fosters a '"knowing" audience', enabling its 'film industry to use songs to activate the culture's cross-referentiality in order to define characters [and] motivate narratives' (2006: 413). Like nearly all stars, Leung does not compose or write lyrics but records others' compositions, both new and traditional. Song lyrics emphasise romantic love but also loss and hardship. Humour figures at times too, as in his repartee with Zhou Xun on 'Cai Qingren' ('猜情人', aka 'Guess Lover') in the antic *The Great Magician*.[25] Overall, Leung's singing activity helps consolidate his star image as a romantic, emotionally vulnerable but easygoing figure. It also helps leaven the impact of Leung's many acting roles that involve his silence, whether as reserved, inexpressive or altogether mute characters (and discussed at other points in this book).

Leung's early career tells a compelling story about continuities and transformations in Hong Kong and regional East Asian entertainment sectors. As key creative figures in screen texts, star actors offer lenses through which to view the practices of complex, transforming industries. Stars' onscreen visibility and the attention devoted to them in the entertainment press allow us to see and interrogate their labour in ways not possible for most industry roles (even the avowedly key role of director, whose labour we apprehend only indirectly). Television series and films put at least some of their actors' work in plain sight. Subject to TVB practices during his training and contract work there, Leung's labour is onscreen plentifully for many years, seeding a longer and even more varied film career as well as a presence in popular music. Leung's global screen stardom begins not with recognition of late 1980s and 1990s genre and art cinema but with acclaim for his prolific, diverse acting in widely circulating TVB series. His rigorous schedule and breadth of roles prepare him well for decades of celebrated work in multiple industrial environments and production categories.

# 3 PAN-ASIAN AND GLOBAL ART-CINEMA STARDOM

Most filmgoers outside East Asia and its global diaspora first (or only) encounter Tony Leung through releases explicitly categorised as art or speciality film rather than popular cinema. Constructed as institution, critical formation or textual category, art cinema offers multiple points of engagement for viewers and scholars. While curators, scholars and cinephiles routinely categorise art cinema in terms of major directors, that cinema often depends too on recognisable performers. This chapter investigates Leung as a global art-cinema star. He has acquired an international reputation based on roles in art-cinema efforts from filmmakers such as Wong Kar-Wai, Hou Hsiao-Hsien and Ang Lee. Leung thus appears a popular star in a regional Asian context but a more rarefied, art-cinema performer internationally. In this chapter, I examine conditions affecting Leung's performance in a range of films received as art-cinema works, alongside critical constructions of art cinema's core attributes, to understand actors' positions in the discursive, aesthetic and industrial fields of art cinema. While film scholars and critics have historically approached art cinema in terms of perceived directorial vision, the formal qualities of film texts, and more recently institutional spaces such as arthouse theatres and festivals, actors and stars also contribute substantially to the signification and appeal of art cinema. However overlooked their contributions may be in film discourse and scholarship, performers are essential components of the 'artistry' of art cinema.

Leung has appeared in films with production financing from many different countries (including in the West, the US and France), and many of his works have earned wide theatrical and home-video release as well. Nonetheless, his films have principally been financed by, filmed in, and earned greatest commercial success in East Asian countries and territories, including Hong Kong, Taiwan, mainland China, South Korea and Vietnam. Looking at Leung's move in the 1990s from local Hong Kong cinema to regional Asian productions, in this chapter I approach Leung as a distinctly pan-Asian actor and star. This designation permits consideration of the specific characteristics of Hong Kong's media industries and culture that inform phenomena of stardom. With this organising principle, I then explore Leung's distinct performance strategies in acclaimed films such as *Chungking Express*, *Flowers of Shanghai* (1998), *2046* and *The Grandmaster*, all of which show him using acting tools both consistent with and departing from the repertoire of techniques on display in television series, dramas and genre films. Leung's evolving performance style in art-cinema works further demonstrates his creative flexibility. Moreover, with production taking place across East and Southeast Asia (and for *Happy Together*, in Argentina as well), and with his films circulating particularly at major international festivals, we see continued evidence of Leung's mobility as an actor and star.

## Acting, stars and directors in art cinema

Leung's work across East Asian production contexts contributes to his reputation since the 1990s as a star of the international art cinema, particularly through films' exhibition and promotion at key international festivals such as Cannes. Leung's collaborations with director Wong Kar-Wai account strongly for his international reputation, whether through the US theatrical and home-video reissue of *Chungking Express* (in 1996 and 1998, respectively) from Quentin Tarantino's Rolling Thunder imprint or the critical acclaim for *In the Mood for Love* following its multiple Cannes awards – particularly Leung's for Best Actor – and wide global release.[1] Wong's and other art-cinema films restrict Leung's performances but in doing so contribute to his focused, coherent reputation outside East Asia as a soulful, contemplative man of letters or philosophy.

Scholars have devoted limited attention to art-cinema acting and stardom partly because discourse around film practices characterised as art cinema does not foreground performance. Before proceeding, then, one might reasonably ask: does art cinema have stars? I contend that art cinema can showcase star performers but does not produce stars. (Or more succinctly: yes, but…) However loosely or narrowly defined, art cinema does not markedly participate in the systems of star incubation and promotion that undergird entertainment cinema. Rather than wade deeply into the minefield of defining art cinema, I put forward András Bálint Kovács' explanation. 'When we speak of "art films" as opposed to "commercial entertainment films," we are referring … to certain genres, styles, narrative procedures, distribution networks, production companies, film festivals, film journals, critics, groups of audiences – in short, an institutionalized film practice' (2007: 21). Art cinema's parameters are of course elastic. Producers and distributors hesitate to attach explicit art-cinema labels to work in circulation thanks to the risk of alienating prospective audiences. (In the US, the preferred industry designation has long been 'film'.) Categorisation as art cinema also depends as much on reception context as on textual features. For example, most Hong Kong dramas not explicitly foregrounding genre elements such as Triad characters and extensive gunplay or other action can be received as art cinema in international release, particularly when shown at festivals, in repertory screenings or at boutique theatres.[2] Even at the strictly textual level, Hong Kong cinema's limited narrative redundancy, shifts of tone between comic and tragic, combinations of serious subject matter with periodic juvenilia, and other features specific to local cultural production can all activate viewing strategies that intersect with those accompanying art cinema.

Overseas film festivals routinely situate Hong Kong and other East Asian films as art products, even when those films circulate in their producing regions as mainstream multiplex entertainment. Festivals provide destinations for both mainstream and releases from producers outside entertainment hubs such as Hollywood. Often organised around auteur worship, festivals contribute to the manufacture and maintenance of star directors. Performers are instrumental to the red-carpet glamour of major festivals such as Cannes and Venice, but are hardly an engine of festival discourse comparable to directors. Festival acting awards routinely go to performers in films legible as art cinema (and such awards contribute to that categorisation too). Festival recognition builds performers' reputations, often as a means for them to gain leverage in wider movie culture. For example, in the wake of her five festival awards (and an Oscar) for her lead role in *La Vie en Rose* (2007), French actress Marion Cotillard moved from work almost exclusively in French cinema to multiple roles in US studio productions, including *Public Enemies* (2009), *Inception* (2010) and *The Dark Knight Rises* (2012). While celebrated again for her starring role in designated auteur director Jacques Audiard's *Rust & Bone* (2012), she now enjoys a reputation as a movie star and not a discrete French-cinema or art-cinema figure.

The international reputations of most stars outside Hollywood cinema depend on circulation of a limited range of works, those films perceived as most competitive in the niche category of foreign film, which in practice refers to – or is received by default as – art cinema. Cotillard, for example, prior to *La Vie en Rose* appeared in more than thirty domestic French productions, with few aside from the Luc Besson–produced *Taxi* series (1998–2007) earning more than piecemeal release outside French-speaking countries.[3] Meanwhile, our subject, Tony Leung Chiu-Wai, has appeared in more than seventy films in Hong Kong and elsewhere in East and Southeast Asia. In English-language venues such as IMDB user forums, reviews of some of his 1980s and 1990s Hong Kong television series and films include assertions such as 'Tony Leung as you've never seen him before',[4] presuming fellow readers' lack of familiarity with titles outside popular genre releases such as *Hero* and *Infernal Affairs*, and in global art cinema, pop-art works such as *Chungking Express* and the drama *In the Mood for Love*. Including and after his television work, though, Leung, as we have seen, has played scores of roles in a multitude of genres, as a lead or co-star in downbeat dramas and crime films, cartoonish action and martial-arts films, and featherweight romantic comedies. Nonetheless, his international reputation is as an art-cinema star, thanks to attention in English-language cinephile discourse to his nuanced romantic roles in films from acclaimed East Asian art-cinema directors such as Wong, Hou and Lee, in works ranging from Stanley Kwan's *Love Unto Waste* and Hou's *A City of Sadness* and *Flowers of Shanghai* to high-profile international releases such as Lee's *Lust, Caution* and Wong's *The Grandmaster*. Distinctions between local tastes and the peculiarities of transnational distribution mean that national and regional cinemas are stocked with actors who earn broad acclaim at home but acquire more rarefied reputations elsewhere. In Italian cinema, for example, another popular star with a dual standing, Marcello Mastroianni, appeared in well over 100 popular Italian films but remains best known internationally for leading roles in ostensible art-cinema works such as Federico Fellini's *La Dolce Vita* (1960) and *8 ½* (1963). Leung enjoys (or contends with) a similarly bifurcated reputation.

Unfamiliar locations and cultural referents, differing performance codes, subtitles or other evidence of linguistic difference such as obvious voice dubbing,[5] storytelling devices, film pacing and other aesthetic conventions can all code even popular entertainments as foreign, exotic and implicitly art products when they circulate beyond domestic or diasporic contexts. Exhibition sites such as festivals and arthouse cinemas can also reframe mainstream genre films as works of high cultural (or subcultural) capital. Colin Hoskins and Rolf Mirus (1988) have noted the 'cultural discount' accompanying non-Hollywood films in international release, but we might recognise a corollary *cultural premium* as well. A given 'foreign' film may not be able to compete economically with its domestic equivalent, but it grants cultural capital to exhibitors and viewers. To the extent that performers are recognised as part of films' key signifying elements, they can secure such capital as well. However, numerous factors inhibit this recognition.

Actors whose work circulates internationally face not only cultural discounts but also relative anonymity. As Jacqueline Reich observes in her book on Mastroianni, stars in nations such as Italy, unlike in Hollywood, must cope with 'the lack of a coordinated public relations institution to help promote and circulate the star persona' (2004: 19). Even more than in mid-sized national cinemas, international art cinema, like much transnational film, encounters a similar challenge, with prospective audiences and publicity channels to reach them spread unevenly across the globe. Many stars appearing in art cinema have agents: Leung, for example, is repped by the large Los Angeles based agency William Morris Endeavor Entertainment. Still, no systematic public-relations apparatus exists to promote art-cinema talent internationally. In contrast to Hollywood stars, whose bankability can be measured explicitly by the box-office figures of films in which they appear, stars' value for art cinema resists quantification. With star appearances often tied to festival screenings that return no revenue to distributors, no statistics exist to prove that a particular star could 'open' an art-cinema release. As a cause or consequence, film-cultural discourse has not framed performers as core exploitable elements of global art cinemas (again, in practice a category subsumed into 'foreign film').

If, as Steve Neale has contended, 'Art Cinema, fundamentally, is a mechanism of discrimination' (1981: 37; capitals in original), one sign of this discrimination may be in the elision of its actors' parallel activity in entertainment media. Cases of stars who bridge the popular-film/art-film divide are numerous but hardly the norm in large film industries,[6] and major publicity channels favour actors who appear in high-visibility popular releases. Festival– and niche-market–based art cinemas usually remove star performers from their home territories' publicity apparatuses, steering them into the larger, more anonymous promotional field for all commercial art cinema worldwide. As James Tweedie observes in his work on art cinemas, the film-festival economy 'produce[s] a new form of cosmopolitan identity' – for festival attendees if not screen subjects – 'and trace[s] a new world atlas, where local cultural workers link directly into a global economy of images, often bypassing the intermediaries of the state' (2013: 24). This new, cosmopolitan atlas can free performers from the legacy of typecasting and other limitations domestic industries may impose, but it also distances them from local (and arguably diasporic) fan bases and institutional supports. And if stardom depends on viewers' recognition of a range of comparable performances, festivals' curation and specialist (chiefly elitist) exhibition criteria necessarily circumscribe star identities, limiting such identities to those that viewers can discern through the films and cultural intertexts circulating at festivals. Leung's acquisition of major US talent-agency representation – despite never having appeared in a US film or English-language production – acknowledges that localised star images may neither travel nor translate internationally.

Festival, art-cinema and other channels can create impressions that particular performers work mostly in highbrow productions and modulate their acting accordingly. In the case of Leung, exposure to the actor's art-cinema roles may suggest that he favours performances that are either (or simultaneously) strongly psychologised, understated, ambiguous or highly stylised (in Brechtian or other modernist fashion). As an expansive category, art cinema offers space for a multitude of performance styles, from the studiously affectless to the most ostentatiously Method-like. Nonetheless, numerous textual and reception features associated with an art-cinema aesthetic downplay performance as an area of textual signification. In Steve Neale's much-debated formulation, art films 'are marked by a ... stress on character rather than plot and by an interiorisation of dramatic conflict' (1981: 13). At the same time, Neale finds in films from director Michelangelo Antonioni 'a problematisation of character motivation and a re-balancing of the weight of attention accorded the human figure on the one hand and landscape and decor on the other' (1981: 14). In other words, performers in art cinema can be seen as figures in landscapes, as compositional devices rather than actors. We may take issues with Neale's (not to mention my own) broad claims. In addition, film style does not deprive actors of all agency. Claudia Springer reminds us that 'even in a rapidly edited montage, actors can make choices about how their characters will be seen' (2015: 15). Still, viewing protocols attuned to such features as nonlinear or non-teleological narrative; lack of or ambiguous causality; anti-typological, modernist or otherwise self-reflexive characterisation and performance; de-emphasis of psychology in favour of a thematic or other organising logic; and a general foregrounding of style can all locate performers in competition with other areas of viewer engagement, rather than at the centre of such engagements. While many custodians of cinematic value such as critics' organisations and festivals give annual awards for acting, discourses surrounding the art of cinema have historically relegated film performers to subordinate status. As Paul McDonald observes in his survey of institutional attitudes toward film acting, 'For the pioneering formalists, it was film that produced meaning, not the star' (2004: 24).

Similarly, the initial major academic efforts to define art cinema, from Neale and from David Bordwell, address the function of character but never mention performance (though Neale does in passing refer to 'gesture and ... vocal delivery' [1981: 31]).

Investigating perceived creators, Bordwell argues that 'the art cinema foregrounds the *author* as a structure in the film's system' (1999 [1979]: 719; emphasis in original). Auteur criticism of the sort Bordwell surveys concerns itself with directors' commanding role in shaping filmic signification, though pays little heed to the major work of directing: that is, directing *actors*. Instead, in art-cinema reception, 'what is essential is that the art film be read as the work of an expressive individual' (Bordwell 1999 [1979]: 720) – the expressive force being an offscreen figure, the director, not those creative agents visible onscreen. Discourse around art cinema does acknowledge sustained director–actor collaborations – François Truffaut's with Jean-Pierre Leaud, for example, or Wong Kar-Wai's with Leung – but even here directors emerge in critical formations as the major expressive forces and drivers of signification.

Through films' circulation at international festivals and their reception in other cinephile communities, directors' reputations contribute to framings of actors, just as star reputations can influence those of directors. Similarly, when approaching screen performance, we can recognize directors as instrumental to (if not entirely delimiting) actors' creative choices, and as co-determinants of the significations of actors and characters. Art cinema as a mode has historically privileged its directors, not least in critical constructions and reception that allude to a rarely explicit directorial vision. Paradoxically, because actors' efforts (or at least the portion of them retained after editing) are visible onscreen, while directors' are fundamentally invisible (in that films do not show us directors working, only the results of that work), art-cinema commentators have tended to overlook screen acting. Compared to the infinite interpretive possibilities available in the gap between filmmaker and text, the apparent obviousness of acting leaves little room for critical embellishment. However, as this book's focus is the actor Leung, not the widely documented work of filmmakers such as Wong Kar-Wai and Hou Hsiao-Hsien, my analysis privileges the actor as the central causal agent of performances and character signification.

By repeatedly casting Leung as a leading man in thoughtful anti-romances that pose questions about Hong Kong's local identity as well as its world position, Wong has been responsible for much of the global awareness of Leung beyond the Chinese diaspora. However, as accounts from collaborators such as Leung and cinematographer Christopher Doyle attest, Wong's creative practice is sufficiently idiosyncratic to defy reasoned analysis. Recalling the production of *Happy Together*, for example, Doyle touches on Wong's desire to showcase his actors while taxing them to the point of exhaustion. One of Doyle's diary entries, titled 'Tony's Presence', reads: 'Wong wants me to give Tony more presence: "He's so unfocused and so de-energized these days." No-one dares tell WKW that four months [in Argentina] has done that to him – and to the rest of us as well' (Doyle 1998: 176). Leung elsewhere recounts further evidence of Wong's oblique or contradictory pronouncements.[7] Perhaps most significantly, then, we can regard Wong's direction as contributing to Leung's ability to perform ambiguity. This ambiguity makes Leung's characters in films from Wong and other directors a productive source of textual instability, and at times a locus for contestation of social norms and state-sanctioned ideologies.

Leung has worked with scores of directors in television and film. While space does not permit in-depth glossing of each collaboration, his performances in films from directors discursively anointed as auteurs show some consistency. As I discuss below, his two films with Hou Hsiao-Hsien, *City of Sadness* and *Flowers of Shanghai*, both involve highly interiorised performances, with limited movement (to accommodate the director's preference for static figures) and little or no dialogue. Contrastingly, in his collaborations with John Woo, for war and action films – *Bullet in the Head* (1990), *Hard-Boiled* and *Red Cliff* – Leung plays characters who reluctantly accede to the violent demands of their positions but, through expression or intimation of sadness or melancholia, evidence a yearning for a world without violence. In thus embodying films' thematics (as I also discuss further in

Chapter 4 with respect to *Hero* and other films), Leung's characters become proxies for Woo, who in interviews has repeatedly claimed that his violent action films at their core thematise the pursuit of peace. While far more mobile and exteriorised than in Hou's films, Leung's characters in Woo's work are not so much active as reactive, negotiating violence that others initiate. And in his most storied and extensive collaboration, in his seven films to date with Wong Kar-Wai, Leung steers a middle course between the physically static characters of Hou's films and the reluctant warriors of Woo's. As I note later too, Leung's performances work to reconcile contradictions Wong builds into characters: from *Days of Being Wild*'s card player readying in his tiny room for a night out, to the courteous beat policeman oblivious to Faye Wong's charms in *Chungking Express*, to *Ashes of Time*'s swordsman going blind, to *Happy Together*'s estranged but devoted boyfriend, to *In the Mood for Love*'s cuckold who believes in love, to the calculating if not particularly successful seducer of *2046*, to the married yet subtly lovesick kung fu scholar of *The Grandmaster*. Leung's acting of these roles combines enigmatic expressions and purposeful silences; gestures that convey reserve, care or good breeding; and occasional flashes of warmth, mischievousness or desire. His performances, usually if not always with the indeterminate 'presence' for which Wong values him, both smooth out and accentuate the ambiguities of Wong's storytelling and direction. Collaborating with other art-cinema directors as well as genre specialists, Leung occupies or commands screen space in alluring, sometimes allusive ways.

## Art-cinema form and performative coherence

To redress inattention to acting in film theory and criticism, and to move from the hypothetical to the embodied, I now look closely at some of Leung's performances in films positioned or recognised as art cinema. As for other actors with varied careers, journalists routinely call upon Leung to distinguish his work in popular and cinemas. A 2000 profile in Singapore's *Straits Times* frames him as 'one of those prolific and eclectic actors who straddles the art-house–mainstream divide', prompting him to respond that 'I see mainstream movies as training. I don't separate my work into art and mainstream. I see them all as opportunities to try out new methods' (Tong 2000). The following year, a feature in the Asian-American focused magazine *Giant Robot* asks him, 'Is it easy to make transitions from an action movie to a comedy to an art movie? You're in every genre.' Again, Leung both acknowledges and downplays the distinction, claiming that 'Actually it's not that difficult. Hong Kong actors – they can do everything. They are crazy' (Wong and Nakamura 2001). His points are *prima facie* contradictory, with moves among different cinema modes simultaneously 'not difficult' and 'crazy', the latter suggesting substantial challenges. The discrepancy can be resolved by accepting the characterisation of Hong Kong actors as unusually versatile, and accustomed to an otherwise difficult process. Though perhaps guided by interviewers' framing questions, Leung's formulations preserve impressions of difference even as they argue for continuity.

Comparing performances in popular and art-cinema works demonstrates that actors modulate their body language and facial expressions to suit the respective material. Compositional, lighting and other formal choices also frame performances in particular contexts. Language deserves attention too, though for East Asian actors, assessing language is a complicated task. Hong Kong cinema's historical practice involved all diegetic sound being recorded after filming (a consequence of restrictive budgets as well as the difficulties of maintaining quiet on any location production in noisy, densely populated Hong Kong). And even before the 2003 Closer Economic Partnership Agreement (CEPA) linking Hong Kong and mainland production, many Cantonese-speaking actors from Hong Kong worked in mainland productions despite limited or no fluency in Mandarin, and vice versa. Mainland releases of Hong Kong productions often include Mandarin dubbing (or revoicing) from other actors. Occasionally, multiple languages share the same space: in *2046* and *The Grandmaster*, for example, co-stars Leung and Zhang Ziyi speak to each other across the film in Cantonese and Mandarin, respectively. Historical reality does lend the choice a measure of authenticity, given the characters' separate Hong Kong and mainland origins (or Canton province for *The Grandmaster*'s Ip Man), if still puzzling for viewers accustomed to relative consistency in film conversations. At the border of genre and art cinema, East Asian and other films periodically include multiple languages without explanation. For example, Zhang speaks Mandarin for most of her lead role in the otherwise Japanese-language *Princess Raccoon* (2005), and Japanese characters apparently understand her. We might recall too the practice in much European film of the 1960s and 1970s, in which all actors speak in their native languages and are dubbed separately for different linguistic markets. In any context, actors who work together onscreen despite not sharing a language face performance challenges in anticipating and responding to their co-stars' words as well as their timing and intonation. Because Hong Kong's production practice involves postsynchronised sound even for local Cantonese releases, and revoicing usually from other actors for regional releases in mainland China and elsewhere, Leung's body and face often supersede voice and language as signifying devices. With pre-release dubbing by an anonymous voice actor a possibility for most of Leung's roles, voice and language become unreliable in reception, no longer indexically tethered to Leung's own performance. In search of stable markers of character subjectivity, viewers accustomed to the frequent revoicing of Leung's characters can build their conceptions of him as actor and character instead on nonverbal performance signs. Thus, across this book I devote considerable attention to Leung's expressions and gestural language – not least in art cinema, a mode that otherwise might not be expected to privilege highly physical characterisations.

Amid a range of formal and industrial practices, varying aspects of Leung's performances code him alternately as a popular or art-cinema figure. His 1980s television roles in urban comedies, police dramas and historical martial-arts narratives involved dynamic body movements and facial expressiveness, as do many of his roles in 1980s and 1990s films. Films such as *Bullet in the Head*, *Hard-Boiled* and *Butterfly and Sword* (1993) equip him with guns or swords, for example, while the fantasies *A Chinese Ghost Story III* and *The Magic Crane* (1993) include scenes of his young monk or martial-artist characters fleeing in comic terror. His many other comic roles, in films such as *Happy-Go-Lucky*, *I Love Maria* and *The Royal Scoundrel* (1991), also involve much facial and gestural clowning. Recall Wong Kar-Wai's assertion (cited in Chapter 1) that before the late 1990s, Leung 'did not quite know how to utilize his body'. Leung does of course use his body as an acting tool in 1980s and 1990s screen roles, if arguably in a broadly theatrical manner, with an expansive rather than restrained gestural language.

A mirror shot in *In the Mood for Love* (2001) restricts Leung's performance while doubling his image

Comparatively, his art-cinema roles often call for understated performances, with minimal movement and limited facial expressiveness. Often essentially paralysed by romantic longing, his characters routinely convey emotion with the eyes and mouth, not with demonstrative gestures or language. Formal choices sometimes dictate the breadth of performance possible. Vivian Lee, writing about *In the Mood for Love*, observes that 'the camera favors close-ups on a character facing the extreme left or right of the frame' and, without 'two-shots or eyeline matches, visual imbalance interrupts the dialogue as a means of communication' (2009: 33). The not-quite-a-sequel *2046* similarly films Leung often at frame edges, far away from his co-stars, and perhaps acting alone rather than in scenes with two cameras covering the performances. Lee's analysis of *In the Mood for Love* foregrounds the viewing experience, arguing that 'close-ups and framing … impose on us a denaturalized vision of parts, rather than wholes' (2009: 33). Single-camera shooting of such visual interruptions also affects performance, with actors performing with fragments of their bodies as well as in fragments of time and space. For production of Wong's films, fragmentation occurs in other ways too. *Ashes of Time*, *2046* and *The Grandmaster* were all filmed in increments over multiple years, with the director favouring improvisation but posing challenges to actors' schedules and any efforts to sustain consistent characters across a discrete production timetable. Remarking on *In the Mood for Love* and *2046*, Lee notes that:

Given that the two films were made almost at the same time, the over-drawn production schedule [of *2046*] put exorbitant demands on the lead actors, especially Tony Leung, as he was asked to play 'the same man [as his *In the Mood for Love* character] in a different way'. (2009: 37; quoting Leung)

Shooting schedules for Wong's film make particular offscreen demands of Leung as a performer. He faces further challenges of duration onscreen as well. In scenes in numerous

Leung mirrored again in a restaurant scene in *2046* (2004)

of Wong's films, Leung performs amid an elongated temporality, with time subjectively extended through fixed-camera long takes or through overcranking. In other films too, dense or deliberately imbalanced compositions from cinematographer Christopher Doyle and others call on Leung to pose in semi-stasis. In *2046*, for example, a flirtation scene with Zhang Ziyi's character includes many choke shots and internal framings, limiting actors' movements. Numerous shots also place Leung or co-star Faye Wong alongside reflective surfaces, creating alluring double images but also requiring the actors' immobility. Here and in other films also, low, sculpted lighting often puts Leung's body and parts of his face in deep shadow, restricting his visible performance to small eye and facial movements. In the 1995 Vietnamese film *Cyclo*, for example, he plays a nearly silent poet (and sometimes knife-wielding gangland enforcer) who spends much time alone in or just outside his small apartment, moving little. In *Cyclo*, shots of Leung from behind or above also repeatedly thwart viewers' efforts to read his character. The shot from behind is a commonplace in Wong's films too. *In the Mood for Love*, *2046* and *The Grandmaster*, for example, all present many sustained shots of the back of Leung's head, emphasising his glistening, pomaded black hair. (*Chungking Express* and *Happy Together* offer such shots as well.) Though these films do allow views of Leung's face and sometimes his body, often in warmly lit settings that magnify his good looks and star charisma, they restrict his performative tools even as they offer him other layers of characterisation as compensation.

Consider *2046*'s just-mentioned flirtation scene. Leung's Chow Mo-Wan character chats briefly with Zhang's Bai Ling after apparently sensing her watching him from the doorway of her apartment. Recognising that he is the object of her gaze, Mo-Wan performs a stylised look of his own. He turns toward her but first directs his eyes downward, then moves slowly to the right of the screen while raising his eyes to meet hers (meanwhile, the camera pans right, moving him to the left of the frame). Finally, the camera pauses with Mo-Wan framed in close-up at screen left, where he unreels a sly smile and says, 'Looking for me?' The fluid camera movement belies the complexity of the scene's blocking,

At Angkor Wat in Cambodia. Leung shot from the rear and positioned at the edge of the frame in *In the Mood for Love*

which partly determines where Leung can move and stand. Next in the scene, Ling undermines Mo-Wan's cool-pose moment by yanking his newspaper-editor friend out from inside her room (where he's accidentally arrived thanks to a prank of Mo-Wan's). In an immediate follow-up scene, Mo-Wan appears again in the same corridor, visiting Ling's room to apologise to her. Here he initially leans casually against the doorframe, again smiling and planted firmly at screen left. He enters her room to continue the conversation and tries to force a gift into her hands, to which she responds by slapping him. The camera lingers on Mo-Wan in a centre-framed close-up in profile, a look simultaneously of detachment and disappointment on his face. Still in this shot, his smile returns, and he resumes speaking to Ling in low tones. The scene also includes two cutaways to Mo-Wan and Ling's hands, the first as he tries to wrap her hands around the gift package, the second as he repeats the gesture later, first clutching one of her hands tenderly, then reassuringly patting the other. Across the scene, tight shots of Leung's face and hands indicate his composure, maintained with minimal apparent effort even

As womanising writer Chow Mo-Wan, Leung flirts with a neighbour in *2046*

when confronted with Ling's feistiness and anger. Other shots in the scene internally frame Leung and Zhang within a tight diagonal arch, also showing Leung entirely from behind. Here the art-cinema aesthetic restricts actors' motion and overall visibility. As for much of the film, though, the scene's abundance of facial close-ups gives its principals opportunities to act in minimal ways, relying on microexpressions and often speaking softly.

The difficult balance between underplaying and not registering at all may be most evident in *The Grandmaster*, where Leung arguably does not so much perform as occupy space. Despite his avowedly extensive, physically demanding kung fu training for his role in the film as martial-arts legend Ip Man, Leung appears onscreen as a mostly static figure, less deeply contemplative than simply withdrawn. Perhaps consequently, Leung's performance, again obeying the compositional demands that Wong's films place on their casts, did not earn the abundance of awards or nominations that regularly greets his work. Leung has long recognised the limited autonomy even of A-list stars. In a 2005 interview, for example, he hints at the lack of freedom afforded actors: 'I think being an actor is quite passive, because you have to follow the director's instructions' (Nochimson 2005: 17).

Whether or not constrained by director instructions, Leung's initial scenes in *The Grandmaster* further indicate the strategies that accompany art-film performance. The film's opening scene includes a stylised one-versus-many fight, with Leung's protagonist Ip Man facing off in a rainy, inky-black alley first against a large group of adversaries, then just one after he swiftly dispatches most of the bunch. Following the scene's establishing shots, the film cross-cuts to a different location, apparently a teahouse or restaurant, to show Ip Man delivering a short monologue on kung fu philosophy. This 30-second insert provides the film's first dialogue, setting up some of the story's themes and presenting modest character texture before returning to the fight scene, which includes no dialogue and many shots with characters' faces either obscured or far from the camera. The insert shows Ip Man in the same wide-brimmed white hat he wears in the intercut fight, a distinctive chromatic touch for that otherwise largely monochrome scene. The insert films Leung entirely in close-up, mostly in a tight shot with his face illuminated on the extreme right of the frame, and with shallow focus showing viewers only the blurry outline of another man standing adjacent, within earshot but outside Ip's sightline. The insert comprises two shots, both arcing around Leung while he sits motionless, moving only his arm to drink and pour tea in the first shot (a shot that also blocks him from view when the camera slowly pans across a pillar or partition). Low side lighting illuminates his face; and with the tight view, shallow focus and the background's near-total darkness, Leung performs the scene almost entirely through facial expressions. Though his aphoristic monologue puts speech at centre stage, many viewers do not hear Leung's voice, given the film's dubbing of Cantonese-speaking actors into Mandarin for the most widely seen version, the mainland Chinese release.[8] (The subtitled US release, though, retains varying Cantonese and Mandarin dialogue.[9]) After the opening fight, the film turns to a scene of Ip Man training alone, as he glosses his biography in an expository voice-over. He moves around an ornately appointed chamber, but since he does

Leung as Ip Man, expounding on martial-arts philosophy in The Grandmaster (2013)

not speak, Leung has no opportunity to alter his facial expressions through dialogue. While he has played silent or emotionally remote characters in many art-cinema works, performing a wholly silent character is not the same as performing the silence that accompanies a voice-over interior monologue (particularly if the actor does not know during filming what the content of the overlaid narration will be, as was likely the case for Leung here). Thus, viewers hear Ip Man (if not necessarily Leung himself in the voice-over) reciting his origins, but Leung lacks cues to register any specific utterance on his face or in his body language more generally. We might regard the effect as akin to art-cinema distanciation, though such a tonality may appear at odds with the film's otherwise mostly linear martial-arts, family and not-quite-romance plots.

In an interview printed in The Weinstein Company's production notes for *The Grandmaster*'s US release, Leung offers a literally positive spin on his work in the film, remarking that 'I'm always playing these dark, repressed characters. But this is such a positive, optimistic role. It was very enjoyable' (Weinstein Company 2013). Onscreen, Ip Man's optimism registers on the surface as resilience and will rather than as strongly expressed positivity. Its early insert scene and some others aside, *The Grandmaster* does not showcase Leung's ability to convey emotion, let alone an emotional range. Director Wong and screenwriters Wong, Zou Jingzhi and Xu Haofeng present Ip Man as largely a cipher, a stony-faced embodiment of kung fu virtue. A romance plot of sorts adds texture to the martial-arts narrative, with Ip Man married but also pining minimally for co-star Zhang Ziyi's character, Gong Er. The film's extensive slow motion and its affinity for static character posing represent Leung's Ip Man as solemnly handsome, if not emotionally, psychologically or physically dynamic. Fight scenes are at times kinetic but also favour Ip Man and his comrades or adversaries standing off in frozen postures. While ostensibly a kung fu film, *The Grandmaster* (like Hou Hsiao-Hsien's *The Assassin* [2015] not long after) operates more as a painterly exercise, not an arty kung fu film – à la *Crouching Tiger, Hidden Dragon* (2000) or *Hero* – but an art film *about* kung fu. Tasked with embodying a philosophy rather than a rounded character, Leung brings presence to his more intimate scenes, though arguably recedes amid other bodies and the overall lush mise-en-scène for most of the central plot involving internecine squabbles among martial-arts factions.

Wong's films featuring Leung span more than two decades as well as a variety of narrative and aesthetic choices. Nonetheless, in both on-screen evidence such as shot composition and blocking and extratextual knowledge such as that of Wong's protracted shooting schedules and his idiosyncratic means of directing actors, Wong's films afford Leung a measure of consistency. Uncertainties may abound on set, but each finished product bears the stamp (or scent, to extend Gary Bettinson's metaphor of sensuousness) of a Wong film. For comparison, then, consider Leung's acting in two films overseen by a very different art-cinema filmmaker, Taiwan's Hou Hsiao-Hsien. Leung first worked with Hou for 1989's *A City of Sadness*, a lengthy but not markedly experimental family drama set amid violent political turmoil in 1940s Taiwan (in particular, the 28 February Incident of 1947, in which KMT troops began the massacre of thousands of Taiwanese civilians). Leung played a deaf-mute photographer, a conceit that freed him from the need to recite lines (or be dubbed) in Mandarin or Hokkein, not languages in which he had demonstrated on-screen fluency at the time. Hou avowedly did not initially plan to make Leung's character mute but made the expedient decision given Leung's inability to master Taiwanese dialect during the film's narrow production schedule. This creative choice resonated powerfully with the film's thematics. Leung's character, the photographer Wen-ching, bears witness to and has the ability to document political violence but cannot vocalise his anger or sadness over the mistreatment and death of family and friends. As Agne Serpytyte (2015) observes, Wen-ching's 'inability to express himself and helplessness in the violent turmoil becomes a metaphor for the inability of the Taiwanese people to voice their outrage'. In addition to facilitating this reading of the film, by compelling Leung to play a deaf-mute character, Hou sets a professional challenge for his lead actor, encouraging Leung to develop the character through movements and expressions.[10]

Nearly a decade later, Leung reteamed with Hou for the restrained chamber drama *Flowers of Shanghai*, set entirely within a Shanghai brothel in the 1890s. This time, Hou's creative practices restricted Leung spatially as well as aurally. In addition to the single, interior location, the film maintains a rigorous long-take aesthetic, with each scene playing out in one lengthy camera shot (the first running eight minutes, for example). While the minimal cutting might seem to benefit performers, particularly those trained (unlike Leung) in stage drama, near-constant camera movement also distinguishes the film. Slow pans back and forth explore the ornate, amber-lit chambers in which action (or more precisely, dialogue) transpires, resulting in shifting character and visual emphasis, with the camera often moving pendulum-like back to a central position.

Sporting a half-shaved head and traditional, loose-fitting robes, Leung occupies the ostensible lead role as Master Wang, an avid brothel patron who spends his time there eating, drinking, playing mahjong and smoking opium (and one presumes, having sex as well, though the film shows no particular interest in lustful, physical displays). In his *Variety* review, Derek Elley (1998) writes of Leung's role that 'Though he never dominates the movie, Wang's character is the hub from which the other characters fan out'. For much of the film, Leung sits calmly while other characters, particularly prostitutes such as Crimson (Michiko Hada) and Jasmin (Vicky Wei), vying for his attention, move and speak around him. His narrative and visual centrality also allow him to speak lines softly, even in whispers viewers cannot hear, as well as offscreen, when his dialogue coincides with the camera panning away from him. Practicalities of language ability inform his line readings, which he delivers in Cantonese, while other actors speak (or, as for Hada, are dubbed into) historically accurate Shanghainese dialect. Meanwhile, a persistent opium haze and the paralysis of being caught between two competing women motivate Wang's immobility. Unlike in Wong's films, though, in which even extreme framings allow Leung repeated close-ups that emphasise his subtle facial expressions, *Flowers of Shanghai* films him almost entirely in long shots. As in many other roles in art-cinema works, he also repeatedly appears shot from behind. In one scene midway into the film in which he tries to soothe a petulant Crimson, he plays with his back to the camera for ninety seconds of the shot, including a full minute spent bent over in his chair, so that viewers see only a formless mass of embroidered cloth at the centre of the frame.

*Flowers of Shanghai*'s blocking and performances choices, while far removed from the dynamic physicality of Leung's many genre roles (particularly in films and series with martial-arts content), call attention to the psychological nature of Wang's agency and his passive demeanour around the opposite sex, as one might expect for an opiated brothel patron surrounded by women whose explicit role is to please him. In the following scene, a slow dolly-in shot finally leaves Leung and Hada visible in a medium close-up, with both seated as he serves her a bowl of congee. As the camera pushes in, other servants orbit around the pair, periodically crossing in front of them, and Leung moves only a few feet in the scene. This limited movement concentrates emphasis on his mannered gestures and his solicitous serving of food to Crimson (who we might remember is the enslaved worker in this scenario, not Wang). While everyone in *Flowers of Shanghai*'s cast abides by the film's formal rigour, the freer movement of characters such as prostitutes, madams and other servants lets Leung establish a quiet presence without needing to be overly demonstrative. His general restraint also underscores the extremity of a violent, scenery-smashing tantrum that arguably provides the film's dramatic climax. When he can narrow his performance to small expressions and careful gestures, any intensification emerges as a dramatic revelation.

## Reading protocols for global art and the local popular

Looking across Leung's extensive, sometimes concentrated filmography – from 1991 to 1994, for example, he starred in an average of six films each year – demonstrates that he has given numerous understated and exaggerated performances in alternation. As noted, most of these films did not receive widespread international release. Local viewers in Hong Kong have enjoyed the greatest exposure to Leung's breadth of work, as well as to news of his offscreen persona. Addressing the particularities of Hong Kong stardom, Leung Wing-Fai stresses that as a result of local media's foregrounding of gossip in entertainment coverage, 'stars' extra-screen presence as celebrity is a central characteristic of their existence' (2015: 47). Meanwhile, art cinema does not offer an organising frame for most Hong Kong viewing constituencies, per Leung Wing-Fai's further observation of 'the limited presence of an art cinema or other non-mainstream media practices in Hong Kong' (2015: 119). Virtually all local films thus enter the market as prospective mainstream entertainments, a factor that may partly explain the limited success of Wong's films in his home territory. At the same time, this lack of distinction means that local viewers do not necessarily frame formally unconventional works as rarefied, high-art objects. Filmmakers and scholars may likewise approach the works and their casts without the hierarchies that undergird reception of works discursively framed as art cinema. Writing on Wong's *Ashes of Time*, for example, Wimal Dissanayake argues that the filmmaker 'plays the public persona of his actors and actresses against the grain of his projected characters' (2003: 69), creating intertextual tensions accordingly. Dissanayake does not specify attributes of any of these performers' public personas, but we might note that in any case, viewers without access to Asian entertainment news would be unfamiliar with those personas. Dissanayake further argues that Wong steers his cast members toward 'an acting style … that is at once marked by casualness and intensity, attachment and distance, and seriousness and playfulness' (2003: 70). To display such a range of conflicting attributes poses challenges for any performer. Leung and others in Wong's films pursue this complex goal even when confronted with compositional restrictions as well as Wong's practice of entering production without finished screenplays.

An iconic slow-motion shot from *Chungking Express*, with Leung as a policeman, preoccupied with a breakup and thus oblivious to a comely food-counter worker's interest, shows

Leung's restrained approach to art cinema's requirements. In that 20-second shot, Leung (as Officer 663) stands at screen left, leaning against a counter and wall, drinking coffee while staring into the distance. At screen right, the worker, Faye (played by star Faye Wong) leans against the other side of the counter to watch Leung. Though it registers as slow motion, the shot is actually undercranked, apparent from the blurry shapes of people who seem to race in front of the camera.[11] During filming, Leung actually raises his cup and drinks at an even slower pace, as Wong holds completely still, to maintain the effect in playback of slow motion and to bolster the film's thematisation of subjective, psychological time. Both Leung and Wong are nearly motionless in the shot, and they do not make eye contact. Still, each anchors the other's performance, providing an eyeline vector (as Wong does), a balancing visual element, and complementary expressions of world-weary if still youthful contemplation.

With the performances he delivers in the expressive spaces created by Wong, Doyle, Hou and others, Leung has the freedom to disregard convention, to expand his repertoire of acting tools. And while restricted physically by requirements of staging and mentally by particular constructions of character, Leung gains from the art-cinema surround a refined screen persona: that of the sensitive, sensual writer, poet or bon vivant. This romantic – and thanks to many films too, sexual – reputation grants him a powerful international currency. Art cinema can remould, refine or provide counterpoints to star personas established in local or global cinemas. Globally positioned outside channels of mass-entertainment publicity, art cinema upsets the ordinary/ extraordinary tension theorised as central to film-star identity and appeal. I hope this initial reformulation of stardom and performance in art cinema suggests some of the ways distinctive aesthetic registers and industry practices facilitate or inhibit certain acting tools and inform the cultural economy of film stardom. Popular entertainments such as genre films arguably power this economy in more overt ways, as the next chapter's investigation of Leung's genre roles addresses.

# 4 TONY LEUNG AND GENRE STARDOM

As marketable names, attractive or memorable faces and sites for
affective encounters, film stars play key roles in the regional and
global circulation of contemporary cinema, not least for East Asian
films. The previous chapter examined Leung's work as it circulates
in international art-cinema contexts. Stars can also be instrumental
to the worldwide distribution and recognition of particular
genres and cycles. Chow Yun-Fat, for example, served as a de
facto global ambassador for Hong Kong's urban crime cinema in
the 1980s and 1990s; Toshiro Mifune did the same for Japan's
upmarket samurai films in the 1950s and 1960s. This chapter
looks at Leung's acting and stardom in genre films, with particular
attention to those earning international distribution. As stressed
across this book, Leung's voluminous screen résumé locates him
in a multitude of popular genres, as well as films (such as Wong's
and Hou's art-cinema works) that escape familiar genre labels.
This breadth of roles across and beyond genres confirms Leung as
a remarkably flexible actor and star.

Across his career, Leung has shuttled among disparate
roles in television and film, a process made smoother by Hong
Kong cinema's internal mixing of genres. While genre production
routinely involves hybridity and overlap, Hong Kong's popular
genres are notoriously impure. Particularly in the boom years of
the 1980s and early 1990s, many releases not only combine,
for example, action and comedy but also deliver abrupt shifts in
tone from sequence to sequence, with even the darkest

crime drama likely to detour into juvenile comedy, or vice versa. Acting in television series and films that feature such tonal shifts prepares Leung for his extensive work in films that do maintain a more consistent generic address (e.g., drama uninterrupted by comedy, or action unburdened by dramatic introspection). In this chapter, I identify two key strands of Leung's genre roles. The first, action and martial-arts films, encompasses action films with contemporary settings as well as historical *wuxia* films emphasising fantastic swordplay, and with tones ranging from deadly serious to outrageously comic. (Since action and comedy often intersect in Hong Kong popular cinema, I include some comedies in this section too.) The second comprises noir thrillers, some (such as the John Woo–directed *Hard-Boiled*) also legible as action films, with others (including *Infernal Affairs* and *Lust, Caution*) foregrounding narrative tension, character psychology, troubled romance and dense atmosphere over kinetic physicality, action or comedy. Films in both categories have enjoyed international circulation, though despite leading roles in such films as *Tokyo Raiders*, *Hero* and *Red Cliff*, screen discourse grants Leung a global reputation based on art cinema and dramatic thrillers, not on comedy or 'pure' action films. As Sabrina Qiong Yu argues, compared to the generally low cultural status of action and martial-arts films in the West, 'Hong Kong action holds a much more prestigious position in its own film culture' (2012a: 16). In the first section below in particular, critics' uninterest in Leung's genre roles even during publicity for the *wuxia* spectacle *Hero* shows how genre films shape actors' reputations, even if by omission. Because reception discourse contributes substantially to genre definitions and to viewer expectations surrounding acting and character, in this chapter I refer often to discursive framings of Leung in order to understand genre's contribution to his overall reputation as an actor and star.

As emphasised across this book and covered particularly in Chapter 2, Leung's activity in popular cinema and television includes dozens of roles in family dramas and light comedies, particularly from the mid-1980s to the early 2000s. Almost without exception, such films did not circulate theatrically outside Asia. As a comic actor, for example, Leung gives a slapstick-style performance as a bumbling reporter in the sci-fi comedy *I Love Maria* and plays a bumbling swordsman in the martial-arts comedy *The Eagle Shooting Heroes*. At the more louche end of his performing spectrum, Leung plays a supporting role as a flamboyant gay man in the 1999 Jackie Chan vehicle *Gorgeous*, and in 2001's *Love Me, Love My Money*, he plays a comic cad in the Hugh Grant mould. Many of these films mine his ladies'-man persona and his capacity for geniality and wry self-mockery. More than demonstrating Leung's range as an actor, such roles suggest the limits of intertextuality in global markets. Evidence of Leung's comic and action roles is explicitly suppressed in promotion of films that showcase Tony Leung, soulful romantic icon, for audiences outside Asia. Meanwhile, many viewers in Hong Kong and the Chinese diaspora still associate Leung with his popular roles in his numerous 1980s TVB television series, series incorporating generic attributes of *wuxia* action, comedy and drama. Consequently, Hong Kong and other East Asian audiences' prefigurations of stars such as Leung contribute to diverse reading strategies. Cinephile viewers outside Asia, on the other hand, recognise Leung principally in terms of the cultural capital his festival awards and ostensible art-film roles provide.

English-language publications can manage to overlook Leung's extensive career even while acknowledging it. For example, the blurb accompanying Leung's entry in *People* magazine's 'Sexiest Men Alive' roundup in 2000 observes that 'In Asia ... he has starred in more than 50 movies and recorded several Top 10 pop hits.' Nonetheless, thanks to his lack of name recognition in the US prior to the relatively high-profile release of *In the Mood for Love*, *People* designates the prolific Leung as 'Sexiest Newcomer' ('Tony Leung Chiu-Wai: Sexiest Newcomer', 2000). In this chapter, I too focus on films of Leung that enjoy some degree of international theatrical circulation. However, I regularly refer to Leung's many roles in expressly local screen texts such as Hong Kong comedies and dramas to highlight aspects of his filmography rendered invisible in wider contexts. Witness the comparative visibility of Leung's work in local context, as with the 2001 Hong Kong International Film Festival's press release announcing a film series devoted to his films:

Tony Leung is the 'Actor in Focus' in this year's Hong Kong International Film Festival. Twelve of his films will be shown: *Chungking Express*, *Happy Together*, *In the Mood for Love* directed by Wong Karwai; *City of Sadness*, *Flowers of Shanghai* by Hou Hsiaohsien; *Cyclo* by Tran Anh Hung; *Tom, Dick and Hairy* by Lee Chingai and Peter Chan; *The Days of Being Dumb* by Kor Sauleung; *Bullet in the Head* by John Woo; *My Heart Is That Eternal Rose* by Patrick Tam; *People's Hero* by Derek Yee; and *Love Unto Waste* by Stanley Kwan. ('Interview with Tony Leung', 2001)

Unlike the selections of Leung's films that screen at festivals such as Cannes and Toronto, those in the HKIFF retrospective include not just internationally distributed films from anointed auteur directors (Wong and Hou most prominently at the time) but also local action dramas and comedies such as heroic-bloodshed melodrama *My Heart Is That Eternal Rose* (1989), with the third-billed Leung playing a loyal friend and romantic interest, and broad Triad comedy *The Days of Being Dumb*, with Leung as half of a hapless gangster duo. As for much of Leung's Hong Kong work, these latter two films' limited circulation prevents them from being name-checked in English-language appraisals.

## Action, martial-arts and *wuxia* films in circulation

While the bulk of Hong Kong productions earn notice chiefly in local entertainment news, Leung's work in globally circulating genre films affords him a degree of visibility in global media discourses. Such publicity has not always been to his advantage, though. For example, in an interview published before the release of *Hero*, co-star Leung (who receives second billing in the film, behind Jet Li) alluded to the film's 'message of peace and human kindness', then expressed support for the contemporary Chinese government's 1989 crackdown on Tiananmen Square demonstrators, claiming that 'What the Chinese government did was right – to maintain stability, which was good for everybody' (Moy 2002). Hong Kong human-rights activists subsequently criticised Leung, and in a later interview the night of *Hero*'s Hong Kong premiere, he tried to contextualise his remarks: 'I'm just an actor. My interest is in making movies, not politics. When I was doing the interview, I was trying to talk from the perspective of [*Hero* character] Broken Sword. It was not my personal viewpoint' ('Tony Leung Chiu-Wai Claims He Was Misquoted Regarding Tiananmen', 2002). Leung's explanation encouraged an understanding of the acting profession as fundamentally apolitical, yet left open the possibility that films and their representatives participate in political discourses. In its denouement, *Hero* may appear straightforwardly to praise Chinese military imperialism, raising questions about its creators' political sensibilities.[1] Consequently, Leung's ambiguously attributed statement in favour of Chinese 'stability' demonstrates how political debates can be waged, and taken seriously, through entertainment channels. Rarely have Leung's words had such global impact: of the films in which Leung has starred, *Hero* remains the most commercially successful worldwide to date. I turn to *Hero* repeatedly in this section, as it provides an ideal case for investigation of relations among screen stardom, genre and discourse.

*Hero* and other international releases indicate the terms on which media outside Asia frame and receive Leung. Particularly in Western critical discourses, his Chinese ethnicity is a key marker of his star persona. Articles about Leung in English-language entertainment publications define him analogously to classical or contemporary US stars: he becomes 'the Asian Clark Gable',[2] 'the Humphrey Bogart of Chinese cinema' (Oon 2003) or 'Hong Kong's answer to Johnny Depp' (Rose 2004). Such analogies interpolate Leung into the constellation of global film stars while explicitly marking his difference from white, American stars past and present. Coupled with his good looks and lean physique, Leung's Asian heritage facilitates his circulation among Western film viewerships as an unthreatening other and object of fantasy. As the analogies demonstrate, Leung's mild exoticism is easily recuperable within the Hollywood-derived frameworks of star appeal: while his Chineseness distinguishes him as an ethnic other, his choice of roles and romantic chemistry with female co-stars facilitate comparisons to Depp and Gable.

As discussed particularly in Chapter 1, substantial portions of Leung's viewing communities of course do not recognise him in terms of otherness, and may not resort to analogies to understand him. For East Asian viewers, Tony Leung may simply be Tony Leung, or Leung Chiu-Wai (though the 'Chinese Bogart' reference comes courtesy of Singapore's *Straits Times*, aimed at a polyglot readership). Nonetheless, his particular attributes, and English-language journalists' willingness to imagine him as a racially transfigured version of a white Hollywood star, contribute to his successful international critical reception. While these analogies largely obscure Leung's action and martial-arts roles, associations with Hollywood stars known in part for romantic roles also help frame Leung as a key figure in another loose generic category, the Asian arthouse romance.

Paradoxically, Leung can exude romantic appeal while sometimes acting in a gender-neutral style, even in action films. *Hero* uses grooming and costume to link Leung to his female co-stars. Aside from his distinctive facial hair, his character in *Hero*, Broken Sword, is visually almost identical to that of Maggie Cheung's Flying Snow. Both wear loose, full-body robes in colours matching the film's various set pieces, and both have long, black hair that occasionally obscures their features (as in the calligraphy-school sequence, during which scenes show each character pouting alone, flowing locks covering half of each's face).

Flying Snow plays a more active narrative role as well, repeatedly duelling Li's Nameless, remaining a combative revolutionary throughout the film, and traversing physical space more vigorously and more often than does Leung's Broken Sword. In more comic *wuxia* or *wuxia*-inflected films such as *A Chinese Ghost Story III*, *The Eagle Shooting Heroes* and *Hero – Beyond the Boundary of Time*, he plays youthful clowns or cads with both connotatively masculine and feminine attributes: in the first, sometimes running in comic fright from combat; in the third, a brazen womaniser; and spending much of the second with his lips comically disfigured while also improbably imagining himself as a skilled fighter.

Leung's filmography shows breadth but also consistency, with a notable tendency toward roles built on reconciliation of contradictions. Even light-hearted comedies typically illustrate his characters' journey from immaturity to sobriety. *He Ain't Heavy, He's My Father* (1994), for example, sends his bitter-son character back in time to meet his father as a young man (notably, played by the other Tony Leung, Leung Ka-Fai), in order to teach lessons

Long hair both frames and obscures portions of Leung's face in *Hero* (2002)

about filial piety. Similarly, romantic comedies such as *Happy-Go-Lucky* and *Love Me, Love My Money* map his transition from unhappy, dutiful repo man with a conscience to death-defying individualist (in the former) or from shallow cad to devoted lover (in the latter). Dramatic roles with action elements strike this balance most prominently. For example, the action drama *The Royal Scoundrel* presents him as a vulnerable, even childlike cop with a toughly masculine façade, and the *Dog Day Afternoon*–inspired *People's Hero* makes Leung a confused, apologetic bank robber. In all of these, his ability to strike notes of both sweetness and astringency, or both familial warmth and selfish petulance, helps lend his characters coherence and depth.

Leung's role in *Hero* as calligraphy master and sometime anti-imperial revolutionary Broken Sword also exemplifies the tendency to balance contradictory character traits. In one of many flashback sequences, Broken Sword engages in acrobatic swordplay as he and Flying Snow attempt to assassinate the King of Qin (Chen Daoming). In another scene in which archers besiege his school, though, he sits indoors, writing calligraphy in sand while Flying Snow and Nameless ward off the attack. Broken Sword's entanglements with women similarly involve contradictions: the film balances his impulsive tryst with the young Moon (Zhang Ziyi), intended to arouse Flying Snow's jealousy, with others that emphasise his silent devotion to Flying Snow as her lover and fellow would-be assassin. In the film's various flashbacks, he repeatedly allows Flying Snow to stab him fatally, demonstrating not only his avowed commitment to Chinese nationalism but also to a romantic-heroic ideal of male deference to women. Along with the narrative machinations required to combine pacifist/warrior and lover/cad into a single character, Leung's performance enables such combinations. In *Hero*, he is a passive presence, acted upon rather than active. He uses quiet and restrained speech, a body language of small gestures, a casual and confined rather than expansive carriage, and perhaps most prominently, a limited range of facial expressions, dominated by those that convey romantic melancholia. Even the film's combat scenes show Leung performing with this melancholic demeanour, for example in a languid, lake-skirting duel with Nameless, which occurs around the body of the avowedly dead Flying Snow. In contrast, his comic *wuxia* roles involve rapid movement (often scurrying away from danger), broad gestures and excited facial expressions.

Leung's long filmography attests to great variations in character types and performance style, and many films have profitably redeployed apparently incongruous aspects of his screen persona. Thrillers and action films can cast Leung as a passive hero by pairing him with a male star more specifically affiliated with urban-crime or martial-arts film roles (or subordinate him to that co-star, in terms of star power and screen time). His role in *Hero* is a supporting one, with plots involving Broken Sword and Flying Snow filtered through the sensibility of the lead protagonist, Jet Li's Nameless. Broken Sword provides the film's thematic and moral centre, but with his belief that swordsmanship's highest principle is not engaging in swordsmanship at all, someone else must supply the spectacular action that motors the film (and Li adeptly fills that role). Generally in the action films and thrillers in which he co-stars, Leung becomes a focal point for romance or psychological narratives, while other characters traffic in martial-arts or gun violence. In *Hard-Boiled*, for example, Leung plays an undercover policeman masquerading as a killer, but Chow Yun-Fat's cop protagonist, Tequila, dominates screen action. Leung participates in many action sequences but even in the film's extended hospital-siege climax leaves the acrobatic gunplay to Chow. The following year's *Chungking Express* wholly excuses Leung's beat-patrolman character from a first-act thriller plot. A decade later, *Infernal Affairs* also makes him an undercover cop infiltrating a Triad gang, but keeps him at a remove from violence until his death in the film's final moments.

Notably, not all Leung's films sideline him from violence. *Butterfly and Sword*, for example, immerses him fully in *wuxia* spectacle alongside co-stars Donnie Yen and Michelle Yeoh, as do contemporary action films with present-day settings such as *Tokyo Raiders* and *Seoul Raiders*. Particularly before the 2003 CEPA co-production agreement with mainland China, action films and comedies comprised the bulk of Hong Kong's film output. Both too have regularly served as venues for Leung's talents, despite his status as neither trained martial artist nor comedian. As Sabrina Qiong Yu notes further of action in particular, 'Hong Kong action genres play a remarkable role in producing stars; it is hard to find a major Hong Kong star who has never performed in an action-oriented film' (2012a: 16). Action films allow Leung to showcase some of the mannerisms of his 'serious' persona, including brotherly devotion to fellow men, soulful or flirtatious entanglements with female co-stars, and an overall romantic temperament, though with an ability to explode in frustration or anger in a realist, psychologised vein. At the same time, most of his action and martial-arts roles grant him lighter, comic moments as well, making room for sly grins or even absurd mugging, and with other emotions and character psychology heavily exteriorised through expressions, gestures and less tightly controlled body language than in his roles in artier films. In action comedies, for example, *Tokyo Raiders* and its sequel *Seoul Raiders* cast Leung as a Jackie Chan–style comic adventurer who leads a team of young, attractive spies. *Seoul Raiders* in particular draws on Leung's legacy as an action star, presenting him in a near-constant stream of martial-arts fight sequences, his performance sometimes embellished with a stunt double but most often aided only by careful action choreography and his co-stars' timing. Leung's casting in action parts suggests the degree to which Hong Kong and transnational producers regard him as a bankable star capable of diverse roles. Curiously enough, his roles in the *Raiders* films show his overlap with mainstream global star Chan, who had developed his trademark action-comedy persona by the mid-1970s. Meanwhile, Leung, eight years younger than Chan and forty-two years old at the time of *Seoul Raiders*' release, remained viable in the regional East Asian market both as an action star and a romantic lead, as later demonstrated in high-profile releases such as *Red Cliff* and *The Grandmaster*.

In the US, no film to date featuring Leung, apart from *Hero* and *The Grandmaster*, has received wide distribution or played in venues other than arthouse cinemas. Even the truncated 148-minute 'international' cut of *Red Cliff*, a war epic with a name director in John Woo, played at only forty-two US theatres in its widest release and was far from a hit, earning well under $1 million in receipts.[3] Consequently, films that in Hong Kong target general viewerships – in particular, Leung's romantic comedies, comic thrillers and martial-arts films – do not circulate theatrically to the US or Europe. Action films featuring Leung have received showings at repertory cinemas, and such films typically do receive local DVD releases directed at martial-arts fans and Asiaphiles, but comedies without action have not received such releases, nor have comic martial-arts films such as *Lucky Encounter* (1992) and *Chinese Odyssey 2002* (2002) geared to local tastes. This pattern accords with understandings of comedy as a highly localised or regionalised form, difficult to market overseas thanks to cultural differences. The virtual absence of comedy from *Hero*, and from Leung's performance in it, helps position the film within categories – including historical drama, epic romance and spectacular action film – that in practice have circulated globally with relative ease.

Even when taking stock of his popular work, much English-language critical discourse surrounding Leung positions him emphatically as a serious actor rather than a celebrity star. A 2003 *Newsweek* profile asserts that 'The actor's gravitas sets him apart from all the pretty boys, action heroes and slapstick comedians who dominate contemporary Chinese cinema' (Seno 2003). Having thus ignored much of his filmography and his television work, writer Alexandra Seno further opines that Leung 'may be the most serious actor of his generation'. Somewhat incongruously, she then notes the existence of many Tony Leung fan clubs, failing to recognise that fan clubs tend to arise around popular stars irrespective of 'seriousness'. Another English-language feature calls on Leung to address the mainstream/arthouse binary. Interviewer Trish Maunder notes his role in the local success *Tokyo Raiders*, which she describes as a 'commercial film', then asks, 'Do you enjoy making popular films like that, or would you rather spend more time making serious cinema?' (Maunder 2001). 'Serious cinema' is understood as its own reward, while 'popular films' might be a waste of an actor's apparently limited time and talent. Leung both acknowledges and refuses the formulation in his response: 'As an actor I love to work on different projects, not only the art-house movies but also some mainstream movies.'

Critical tunnel vision surrounding actors such as Leung arises from the mainstream/arthouse binary, from related biases about disreputable genres, and from responses to particular modes of performance. The critical bias in favour of dramatic roles, and against comic or action-centred ones, corresponds to a widespread critical preference for ostensibly cerebral rather than accessible performances. Leung's flexible performance style thus produces varying critical responses, ranging from strong affirmation to wholesale neglect. Films lauded in English-language criticism largely showcase Leung's acting in what James Naremore (1988: 28) terms a 'representational' style, a comparatively interiorised style that in theatrical performance attempts to preserve the illusion that no audience is present. Meanwhile, Leung's roles neglected in most English accounts feature him performing in a 'presentational' style (Naremore 1988: 29), which in stage drama explicitly acknowledges the audience and does not depend on realist psychology. In films such as *In the Mood for Love*, *Hero* and even the popular thriller *Infernal Affairs*, Leung acts in the representational mode, conveying psychology through small gestures, facial expressions best viewed in close-up and limited onscreen dialogue. In comic roles such as those of *Tokyo Raiders* and *Chinese Odyssey 2002*, Leung gives presentational performances, playfully acknowledging his characters' comic situations with expansive gestures (including many fight scenes in both), broad smiles, and extensive and often rapid dialogue. As with much broad action and comic performance, such roles may be read (or misread) as having no psychological dimension, and thus demanding limited intellectual engagement from viewers. Leung's work outside action, martial arts and comedy, in a range of popular or highbrow thrillers, often involves highly psychologised characterisations and performance, taking us to the second strand of Leung's transnational filmography.

## Noir thrillers, restrained performance and Leung's international persona

Leung has starred in numerous successful thrillers that deploy a refined noir sensibility, and aspects of his star persona and performances contribute substantially to that sensibility.[4] This section investigates his acting and stardom in his shared leading role in *Infernal Affairs*, with attention to other roles in contemporary films categorisable as noir thrillers, such as *Cyclo*, *Confession of Pain* and *Lust, Caution*. Particularly outside action and martial-arts films or comedies, Leung's performance style lends itself well to transnational circulation. Many of his roles entail limited dialogue, and in numerous films – including *In the Mood for Love*, *Chungking Express*, *Cyclo*, *2046* and more – he delivers monologues in voice-over, freeing him onscreen to act exclusively through facial expressions and body language. Though his 1980s television work locates him in family dramas, broad comedies and martial-arts roles, in 1990s and more recent films released to international critical acclaim he performs in a restrained, highly cinematic manner, relying on a slack posture and in particular his expressive (if often downcast) eyes to convey emotion. His films that travel internationally showcase a narrow range of characterisations and performance attributes. This circumscribed persona distinguishes Leung in the competitive global market for art and prestige cinema and for niche genre releases.

Viewers exposed to Leung's work circulating internationally in the 1990s and 2000s see a reasonably consistent trajectory for his characters: he will mope, desire, suffer, engage in morally dubious acts or even outright criminal ones, and more likely than not die ignominiously. Narrative, cinematography and performance construct his characters in dramatic thrillers as archetypal noir heroes or antiheroes. While numerous generic and other descriptors accompany these films in reception discourse, the terms 'noir' and 'thriller' recur frequently (and often interchangeably) for all of them. Many of Leung's urban action films and thrillers (such as *Hard-Boiled* and *Infernal Affairs*), as well as moody romantic dramas (including *In the Mood for Love* and *2046*), operate as contemporary film noirs narratively, visually and in reception contexts. Such varied film as the lush un-romance *Cyclo*, the bleak cop melodrama *Confession of Pain*, the erotic historical fiction *Lust, Caution* and even the kinetic, avant-pop *Chungking Express* also fit broad categorisations of cinematic thrillers or neo-noirs.[5]

Taken together, Leung's thriller roles have been the most critically successful of his body of work and have earned him repeated accolades at Hong Kong industry awards and international festivals. Many of these films have been among his greatest commercial successes as well, particularly at the local Hong Kong box office. *Infernal Affairs* and its two sequels have been credited with a revitalisation of the Hong Kong film industry at the outset of the twenty-first century,[6] and Leung's regional and global star power represents a significant component of Hong Kong cinema's transnational disposition. His noir roles show the greatest portability to international festival and arthouse markets. Still, like his overall body of work, some of Leung's noir-tinged roles principally target local Hong Kong and regional East Asian viewerships. *Infernal Affairs*, for example, played only infrequently outside East Asia; and *Confession of Pain*, which teamed him again with *Infernal Affairs* co-directors Lau Wai Keung and Mak Sui Fai (aka Andrew Lau and Alan Mak) and frequent co-star

Takeshi Kaneshiro, received no North American or European theatrical release, screening only at mid-tier festivals. The film's depiction of nighttime Hong Kong as a sea of neon greens and blues, and its stylised flashbacks mixing black and white, colour and sepia tones, offer points of access for style-minded overseas audiences. However, its complicated plot, somewhat impenetrable characterisations and maudlin affect made it a difficult proposition for global distribution. And until recently, even mainland China had not been a prime destination for Leung's noir-inflected films. With the exception of the 2012 espionage drama and Chinese box-office success *The Silent War*, Leung's noir-based films have faced cuts or simply gone unreleased on the mainland, owing to censorship of sexual or crime content perceived as too racy or as not prosocial. For example, while Andy Lau's Triad-affiliated cop eludes justice in the original release of *Infernal Affairs*, the mainland release ends with his character's arrest, adhering to SARFT requirements that official corruption be explicitly punished. (Either way, Leung's character dies.)

Leung's thriller roles contribute to his twin status (discussed in Chapter 3) as a mainstream star in East Asia and an arthouse figure among Western reception communities. The thriller form encompasses the creative labour of filmmakers identified with the East Asian mainstream (e.g., *Infernal Affairs* series directors Lau and Mak), with global art cinema (e.g., Hong Kong's Wong Kar-Wai, Vietnam's Tran Anh Hung, Taiwan's Hou Hsiao-Hsien and others), and with figures regarded as both mainstream and auteurist (in particular John Woo, with whom Leung has worked repeatedly, but also Ang Lee, who directs Leung in *Lust, Caution*). Films' circulation and box office have varied widely by region, though. *Infernal Affairs*, Hong Kong's top-grossing film of 2002, received only a limited release at US and European arthouse cinemas, and not until 2004. The later *Lust, Caution* had its greatest success in East Asian markets, with receipts in China, South Korea, Taiwan and Hong Kong all surpassing North America's, where it played in a total of 143 theatres during its widest release (a substantial number, but far below the 2,000 or more screens on which major Hollywood releases open in the US).[7] These films, and Leung's stardom within them and across his filmography, demonstrates ways that star casting combines with genres such as the thriller or modes such as film noir to position films for distribution in local markets.

To proceed, I offer brief overviews of Leung's role in four films legible as noir thrillers. In *Infernal Affairs*, Leung plays an undercover policeman, Chen Wing Yan, who infiltrates a Triad gang and whose loyalties remain divided between the opposing groups; co-star Andy Lau (aka Lau Tak-Wah), meanwhile, plays Lau Kin Ming, a Triad member who infiltrates the police force. At the film's climax, another policeman kills Yan just before he exposes Ming. Leung plays in new flashback scenes in the sequel *Infernal Affairs 3* (2003), then rejoins much of *Infernal Affairs'* production team for *Confession of Pain*, where he plays Lau Ching Hei, another policeman leading a double life. Hei is at once a mild-mannered husband and a sadistic killer who murders his father-in-law as vengeance for his own family's murder decades earlier; he stalks and plots to murder his own wife as well. His foil in this film is his alcoholic ex-partner, Yau Kin Bong (Kaneshiro), who investigates the father-in-law's death and solves the case. Apparently unconcerned with capture, Hei nonetheless kills himself at the film's denouement when he feels regret for orchestrating his wife's death. Leung followed this gloomy effort with the historical drama *Lust, Caution*, playing Mr Yee, a high-level Chinese-government official collaborating with the Japanese occupation in late 1930s and early 1940s Shanghai. He begins an affair with a young activist, Wong Chia Chi (Tang Wei), who he believes to be Mak Tai Tai, the wife of a wealthy businessman ('Tai Tai' is a colloquial name for a moneyed wife). After Wong alerts Yee to her comrades' plan to assassinate him, he orders the plotters' arrest and execution, as he has done for many others across the film. While Wong's story and subjectivity dominate the film, it closes with a scene of Mr Yee alone and disconsolate.

Finally, we can include Leung's earlier role in *Cyclo* as an unnamed underworld figure, identified in the credits as 'Poet', who moves at the margins of the world of the film's title character, a nameless cyclo driver (Le Van Loc). A mass of contradictions, Leung's character recites poetry in voice-over, romances the cyclo driver's sister (Tran Nu Yên-Khê) while involving her in mildly kinky but mostly sexless prostitution in his apartment, and occasionally ventures out to supervise gruesome acts of knife homicide against criminal adversaries. Before the film's climax he sets his apartment aflame, perishing (offscreen) in the blaze. All four films, then, show Leung's characters pursuing strikingly contradictory activities – policing and crime, sex and killing, poetry and torture – characteristic of noir worlds' ambiguity, irrationality and intensity. In all as well, Leung remains a figure of at least partial sympathy even in the wake of acts of violence and betrayal. Arguably, the films' affective dimensions emerge more from Leung's restrained, interiorised performances than from narrative or other textual cues. As victimiser and victim, authority figure and malefactor, Leung exudes sexual charisma and psychological energy that radiate out to lend noir texture to the films' surrounds.

We can begin chronologically with *Cyclo*, which harnesses varying facets of Leung's acting and stardom for screen art, noir atmospherics and global legibility. His profile in this film sets off his later noir-thriller roles in compelling ways. As in many other films, he does not play the main character, occupying instead a supporting role that defines the film's project. *Cyclo*'s lead figure is its destitute, toiling cyclo driver, while Leung's poet, pimp and torturer embodies the film's uneasy balance of lush aestheticism and graphic violence. Leung performs amid a Ho Chi Minh City milieu of deep, saturated hues, and he enacts his character's and the film's oppositions with what will become his trademark international performance style, that of passionate detachment. His performance constructs a sombre, withdrawn figure ambivalent about his position in the camps of both art and brutality. (Given Leung's apparent lack of mastery of the Vietnamese language,

In *Cyclo* (1995), Leung's brooding poet shot with signature noir obstructions

his nearly wordless performance also conveys the character's detachment, with two poetic voice-overs comprising about half his dialogue in the film.) Leung's casting, here and in later films such as *Hero* and *Lust, Caution*, arguably represents a shrewd manoeuvre on producers' parts, as his minimally demonstrative acting style in dramatic roles allows him to serve as a repository for thematic meanings that in other forms could create substantial textual incoherence.

The poet of *Cyclo* incorporates character traits that Leung also later displays in more commercially successful films that straddle arthouse and multiplex terrain. The reluctant antihero, skilled in violence but loath to use it even when employed in criminal enterprises, partly defines his characters in *Infernal Affairs* and *Lust, Caution*. Similarly, the poet's longing for romantic happiness matches the outlook of most characters on the dramatic side of Leung's filmography. Acting with little or no dialogue also distinguishes his dramatic roles, with narrative conditions often explaining his reticence. Substantive personal and professional issues remain unarticulated in many of his noiresque films, whether owing to social convention (as is the case in *In the Mood for Love*), subterfuge (in *Hard-Boiled* and *Infernal Affairs*) or both (*Confession of Pain* and *Lust, Caution*). Complementing narrative and film style, Leung's performances contribute to the possible categorisation of particular films as noir texts. He repeatedly embodies discontented, alienated and psychologically divided male figures who both belong to and define the milieu of contemporary global noir. Along with narrative machinations and formal choices such as lighting, camerawork and sound, Leung's characterisations contribute substantively to the stylised and romanticised but also pessimistic tones of *Infernal Affairs*, *Lust, Caution* and other dramatic crime and thriller narratives in his filmography. In contemporary cinema, the philosophical, romantically inclined (if doomed) man who inhabits a world of violence is a stock figure in films that cross over between festival/arthouse channels and mainstream theatrical release.

In Hong Kong in particular, noir thematics often foreground a male protagonist defined by a complex, conflicted relationship to his work sphere, his social circle (when he has one) and the wider political environment (often represented obliquely, especially in the post-CEPA era of mainland co-productions). Leung in many films embodies a specific Hong Kong variant of a noir protagonist: a civilised, physically unimposing man who adapts to a world of violence and deceit. In *Infernal Affairs*, while both Leung and Andy Lau play undercover agents (a policeman infiltrating the Triads, and vice versa), Leung comports himself as a soulful New Man with a romantic temperament, exhibiting neither a policeman's disciplined bearing nor a gangster's wary, adrenalinised one.

Lau similarly does not perform as a conventional thug, and even in his policeman guise carries himself more like a toiling bureaucrat than an authority figure. In their few scenes together, Leung and Lau (as characters Yan and Lau) productively contrast each other, with Lau connoting more of a physical threat alongside the slightly shorter, more compact Leung. The film's climactic rooftop confrontation gives Lau more command of space, with

Leung materialising wraithlike behind him, and with Leung's body positioned directly behind Lau's in many shots (with shot selections that emphasise their synchronised stances, though diegetically indicating Yan's use of Lau as a shield). For much of the film, Leung's relaxed body language signals his desire not to occupy fully the spheres of crime or law enforcement, while Lau's coiled posture and occasional furtive gestures accentuate his strain to fit into either realm. Only with Yan's death – which makes good on the film's persistent intimations of fatalism – does Lau appear to become whole, eliminating the officially sanctioned deceiver Yan and thus gaining stature in both his police and Triad guises. Such agency is unstable, though, not least thanks to parallel *Infernal Affairs* texts that put paid to Lau's ambitions: both the mainland-release version of the first film, in which he is arrested following Yan's death, and the sequel *Infernal Affairs 3*, in which Lau's years of deceptions push him toward madness, and in which he is finally bested by another undercover agent, this one an indomitable mainlander played by Chen Daoming.

Early in *Infernal Affairs* (2002), future adversaries Leung and Andy Lau listen contemplatively to music

Leaner still and more angular than Leung, the actor Lau has played not only conflicted noir antiheroes (in such films as 1999's *Running out of Time*, as a noble, terminally ill criminal) but also more conventional, prosocial police characters (for example, in 2013's *Firestorm*). Leung and Lau have played together repeatedly, in 1980s TVB series as well as a handful of early-1990s films, so *Infernal Affairs* builds on their legacy of coordinated performances. The action comedy *Come Fly the Dragon* (1992), for example, pairs Lau and Leung as fighter pilots recruited against Taiwanese arms smugglers, but the film ultimately makes Lau's character the alpha male of the duo, with Leung's still comically effectual but directing his energies toward mischief and romance. In *Infernal Affairs*, Leung's carriage, expressions and intonations draw out the comparatively 'harder' affect of co-star Lau, just as Lau's tightly wound masculinity makes Leung's manhood comparatively more elastic, connoting either fatalistic resignation or a promising ambiguity. Noir masculinity admits a range of types, even in the contained milieu of Hong Kong film, making space too for the amoral antiheroes Leung plays in *The Longest Nite* and *Confession of Pain*. The template Leung provides in *Infernal Affairs* has proven especially robust. Other actors have followed in his path, playing quiet, restrained police detectives whose apparent psychological distance from events and surroundings can represent a practical coping mechanism. For example, conducting a methodical but dispassionate investigation of a young woman's murder in the elliptical neo-noir *Port of Call* (2015), Aaron Kwok takes on a similar role to those Leung plays in many thrillers (if in the newer film with paternal love substituting for any onscreen romance). On Hong Kong screens, principled withdrawal from the wider world – in favour of a concentrated focus on, say, a criminal investigation – offers male professionals a means to negotiate inequality, corruption and the overarching presence of authoritarian mainland China.

The characters Leung plays in thrillers and dramas routinely behave in ways suiting the loosely understood narrative parameters of thrillers and neo-noirs. As the undercover cop Yan in *Infernal Affairs*, Leung must play simultaneously virtuous (his 'real' personality) and criminal (masquerading to maintain the trust of his Triad brethren). He manages these opposing roles through passivity. Yan refrains from explicit violence, and until the film's climax, he never instigates action. In addition, Leung has played many police characters, from virtuous to murderous, as well as numerous men with divided loyalties or ambiguous moral positions. His *Infernal Affairs* role as an undercover cop troubled by his immersion in the criminal world reprises much of the profile of his *Hard-Boiled* character, an assassin who is really a policeman working under deep cover. This thematic thread of psychological duality brings together a substantial portion of Leung's filmography, framing him as both a noir protagonist and a performer who can convey complex emotions. Psychological characterisations, along with emphasis on interior conflict rather than physical action, can fulfil arthouse audiences' expectations for character-based drama rather than propulsive spectacle. At the same time, Leung's performance attributes – for example, his ability to manifest 'presence' with limited or no physical movement – can serve the requirements of such varying genres and modes as romantic drama, martial-arts epic and urban noir thriller. Leung's characters can thus occupy both conventional generic categories and those linked to exhibition sites such as art cinemas.

Circulation of Leung's films, while clearly dependent on genre positionings or lack thereof, also reveals preferences for particular acting styles in international markets. Audiences worldwide often respond to straightforward, uncomplex characterisations and performances. At the same time, critical acclaim and sometimes commercial success also accompany performers who can convey ambiguity through facial expressions and a modest repertoire of body language, and who can communicate psychology, emotion and a range of moral positions nonverbally, in ways resonant in different cultural contexts.

While prevailing industrial and academic wisdom asserts that action genres travel more widely than other film output, in Leung's case dramatic roles and restrained performances in thrillers have circulated more successfully than his action efforts or other physically demonstrative roles. In films such as *In the Mood for Love*, *Infernal Affairs* and *Lust, Caution*, Leung gives highly psychologised, physically restrained performances. *Infernal Affairs* puts him and Lau in a climactic rooftop standoff with guns drawn, but no kinetic gunfight occurs; instead, a circling camera emphasises the protagonists' stasis. *Lust, Caution* locates Leung's character almost entirely in interiors such as parlours and bedrooms. Even in the uncensored version of the film's two lengthy sex scenes, the naked Leung moves very little (partly to shield his genitals from camera view), and his most dynamic physical movement in the film occurs when he rushes into the back seat of a car after learning of a threat to his life. In contrast, in films such as the action-comedy *Tokyo Raiders* or the romantic comedy *Love Me, Love My Money*, Leung's presentational style playfully acknowledges his characters' comic situations with expansive gestures, broad smiles, and continuous and often rapid dialogue.

The global appeal of Leung's illusionistic, representational performances demonstrates not only regional and international taste preferences but also implicit critical patrolling against certain forms of performative expression. After *Hero* and *The Grandmaster*, Leung's most successful starring effort to date in terms of critical recognition and global arthouse circulation has been *Lust, Caution*,[8] the erotic historical drama built on a slow-burning assassination plot and framed in promotional and journalistic discourse in terms of its numerous graphic sex scenes, a rarity in diasporic Chinese cinema. Leung's performance as a sombre man entrapped by his own social position handily merges the lonely, conflicted characters he plays in his many films under director Wong Kar-Wai as well as in genre-driven efforts such as *Infernal Affairs*. Reviewing *Lust, Caution* in the *New York Times*, Manohla Dargis (2007) writes, 'Few actors convey desire as beautifully or with such reserve. ...

In his best films ... Mr. Leung doesn't do much talking: he looks, he conquers.' Her remarks suggest the degree to which restrained performance – characterised by minimal, cinematic expressiveness rather than theatrical gestures or other expansive physical efforts – registers here as more accessible, engaging and overall pleasurable for discerning viewers than do other performance styles. The noir aesthetic of sculpted lighting, dynamic compositions and narratives turning on duplicity and betrayal further promotes restrained, representational performance. Leung's 'soulful' performances – the description features repeatedly in reviews of his work – can anchor viewers in films dominated by complex narratives or dense images of urban space, whether contemporary or historical.

To highlight the consistency of Leung's performance across films that address their audiences in very different ways, I offer for comparison brief moments from *Infernal Affairs* and *Lust, Caution* that make comparable use of Leung while fulfilling distinct dramatic needs. In *Infernal Affairs*, the character Yan spends most of the film in the company of his fellow criminals. Some of these engagements – particularly a scene in which he uses Morse-code finger-tapping to relay information about a drug shipment while in the Triads' company – involve his tense efforts to maintain his cover. Others, though, present his affable, familiar relations with other men. At the film's second-act climax, Yan sees his friend and superior, Superintendent Wong (Anthony Wong), killed by Yan's criminal partners. Yan then escapes the ensuing melee alongside the slow-witted Keung (Chapman To), who is soon revealed to have been fatally shot. Delivering an oblique monologue as the pair drive along a tree-lined country lane and then crash into a ditch, the dying Keung implies that he had known Yan's true identity but kept the secret out of loyalty to his comrade. After this revelation, Yan appears in a tight close-up, with Leung's expressive eyes convening rage, disbelief and sadness, and calling forth a range of signifying possibilities. Leung's face must bear the weight of the scene's (and the film's) complex emotions generated around masculinity and male friendship, around codes of honour and

A tight close-up emphasises Leung's expressive eyes as he reacts to his friend Keung's death in *Infernal Affairs*

betrayal, around deception and knowledge, and around justice, violence and mortality.

*Lust, Caution* also puts Leung at the crossroads of intimacy and betrayal, and production choices focus attention on his eyes and face. Cinematographer Rodrigo Prieto used an amber eyelight on Leung during the film's interrogation scenes: 'We subtly created the effect of embers lighting him during his intense lines. ... It did add a touch of almost terrifying insanity to his gaze' (Chang *et al.* 2007: 254). Technical elements thus steer viewers toward the thematic dimension of Leung's performance, in ways legible without translation. Remarking on another scene, in which Mr Yee acknowledges Wong's love for him solely through facial expressions, editor Tim Squyres observes that 'Leung was given the extraordinarily difficult job of portraying this without being able to say it, and the simplicity and effectiveness of his performance is amazing' (Chang *et al.* 2007: 254). With this praise, Squyres too implicitly asks prospective viewers to accept Leung's face and eyes, not his voice, as the actor's key performance tool.

*Lust, Caution* ends after a brief exchange between Mr Yee and his usually distant wife (Joan Chen), and its penultimate image is also a close-up of the silent Leung. The shot shows Mr Yee alone in the empty bedroom formerly occupied by his consort, Mak (or Wong), whose offscreen execution he has just sanctioned. The image puts Leung off-centre in the frame, dark shadows engulfing the room but leaving his face visible from the eyes down. His off-axis glance into space provides the film's final view of human emotion, his expression serving as the repository for viewer sentiments and interpretive possibilities. (Finally, he steps out of frame, leaving only his shadow set against a rumpled white bedsheet.) Beyond their distinct affective engagements, the two scenes demonstrate that Leung can perform in a similar dramatic register in both local genre films and those with crossover appeal to international arthouse audiences.

*Lust, Caution* is particularly notable in cementing the image of Leung as a soulful romancer trapped in history. Moreover, it extends the darker strand of his persona to depict him as a public

Leung alone and engulfed in shadow in the penultimate shot of *Lust, Caution*

and private villain. When not engaged in connotative rape and other sexual encounters relying on disturbing power imbalances, his character supervises interrogations, torture and executions. For international audiences, Leung's turn in *Lust, Caution* may represent casting against type. In Hong Kong films not circulating widely, Leung has played numerous villains. In 1998's *The Longest Nite*, for example, his corrupt-cop protagonist repeatedly assaults the film's female lead (Maggie Siu), finally shooting her multiple times in the leg, throwing her from a moving car and running her over. Later, in *Confession of Pain*, Leung's policeman character sadistically bludgeons a criminal in the opening scene as his unnerved colleagues watch, numerous scenes revisit his graphic murder of his father-in-law, and the film devotes extensive screen time to his terrorising of his innocent wife. Still, the notion of Leung as an actor associated with sweet characters such as *Chungking Express*'s guileless beat cop or *In the Mood for Love*'s heart-aching writer helps set off his *Lust, Caution* role as daring and remarkable.

Cases such as Leung's demonstrate that markers of acting prestige may compete with and thus undermine star appeals based on associations with popular genres. At the same time, the flexible space of noir – genre or modality; aesthetic register or sensibility; accumulation of narrative markers; and site for coded performances balancing criminality and heart, amorality and devotion, stolidity and sexiness – shows ways critical plaudits and generic structures can consolidate a particular star image. Facilitating his most psychologically intense and interiorised performances, while foregrounding his romantic appeal, noir offers a staging ground for the kind of acting work most favoured in global screen cultures. *Infernal Affairs* and other noir thrillers featuring Leung operate at the intersection of global mainstream cinema, transnational genre releases and implicit arthouse categories of 'foreign' or exotic film. Leung's mutable star persona and the intergeneric apparatuses of cinematic thrillers and neo-noirs speak to multiple constituencies in complex ways. I hope this brief survey of a small number of Leung's many roles in films that strike generic chords has indicated some of the issues raised by regional stars in global circulation. I turn next and finally to Leung's most recent work, also in genre films, specifically those positioned for the growing market in mainland China.

# 5 THE MAINLANDING OF TONY LEUNG CHIU-WAI

While a major transnational star, particularly in regional East Asian cinema and in global festivals and niche-market exhibition, Leung now finds his work most richly supported and exhibited in mainland China. China's cinema market has exploded in the past decade, with a growing slate of increasingly lavish local films, a huge boom in multiplex construction, and a corresponding surge in box-office receipts, particularly for domestic productions (thanks in part to state manipulation of imports and release windows). As mentioned at the start of this book, Leung's most recent roles have been in mainland films that play to nationalist sentiments, films valorising Chinese historical struggles from the dynastic era to the 1940s, never with contemporary settings or onscreen engagements with the West. Long a participant in regional Asian co-productions with companies in places including Taiwan and Vietnam, Leung's last such work was 2005's *Seoul Raiders*, a Hong Kong/South Korea co-production with filming in Hong Kong and Seoul. Aside from a cameo appearance in the Bhutanese/Hong Kong film *Hema Hema: Sing Me a Song While I Wait* (2016), he has since 2007 only appeared in mainland Chinese films or co-productions with mainland companies (the default mode of recent Hong Kong productions following the implementation of the Mainland and Hong Kong Closer Economic Partnership Arrangement [CEPA], first signed in 2003).[1] Leung's once hugely prolific output has slowed, but includes many of China's highest-profile releases. He played the lead in the mainland historical epic *Red Cliff*, director John Woo's return to Asian production; starred in 2011 in another period pageant, the comedy-drama *The Great Magician*; and performed in another lead role as a blind spy in 2012's propagandistic *The Silent War*, a successful prestige release in mainland China that did not receive worldwide theatrical distribution.[2] Most famously in this period, he appeared as martial-arts icon Ip Man in director Wong Kar-Wai's *The Grandmaster*, a China/Hong Kong co-production that received a substantial global release, including at its peak screenings in over 800 North American theatres, where it grossed just over $6.5 million.[3] *The Grandmaster* earned by far its highest receipts – over $45 million of its $64 million global total – in mainland China, clearly indicating where Leung's star presently shines brightest.

The transit from local to international to mainland productions involves numerous markers of stardom and creative practice, variations in acting technique among them. Accordingly, this chapter investigates Leung's choice of roles and modulation of performance style to remain artistically active in Greater China's evolving industrial environment and market. Leung's roles can be viewed as risk-aversion strategies, as cynical capitulations to mainland regulators' preferences, as the burden of major stars' career progression, or as creative strategies to pursue new artistic challenges in his fourth decade of continuous screen acting. Here, I devote attention to Leung's performances in *Red Cliff*, *The Great Magician*, *The Silent War* and *The Grandmaster*. Overall, this chapter draws conclusions about Hong Kong and mainland Chinese industries' management of performing talent, contributing further, I hope, to understandings of the evolving dynamics of interconnected East Asian screen industries and actors' roles within them. While Leung's mainland-linked efforts are distinct in many respects from his previous work, they also further his status as a flexible, mobile and durable actor and star. Working on Mandarin-language releases in the ideologically regulated mainland film industry offers yet more evidence of his professional flexibility. The move to mainland shooting, along with continued location work in other Asian territories, also straightforwardly denotes his mobility. The epic *Red Cliff* included filming outside the mainland, in Taiwan. His previous work, the US/China/Taiwan co-production *Lust, Caution*, involved not only Hong Kong and mainland filming but also location shooting in Malaysia. Finally, as the lead actor in some of mainland China's highest-profile releases, Leung's recent activity demonstrates again the durability of his screen stardom.

Leung's mature career finds him in the midst of the mainlandisation of Greater China's film industry, with Hong Kong no longer the centre of Chinese-language screen production and consequently no longer the principal force shaping the cultural content of films that involve Hong Kong companies and stars. Leung's last film shot exclusively in Hong Kong was 2006's *Confessions of Pain*, with nearly all his subsequent films shot wholly or in part in mainland China.[4] Unlike many Hong Kong film workers, already-popular stars such as Leung enjoy relative privilege in the new system emphasising mainland filming and release (sometimes with filming in Mandarin rather than post-production dubbing). Yiu-Wai Chu cautions that in this new industrial regime, 'only actors and actresses, in particular those who are highly acclaimed, can enter the Mainland market' (2013: 114), with other Hong Kong professionals left behind. The mainland's rise has also dismantled the star-making apparatus once provided by TVB, local film producers and the content-hungry local market, with Chu noting too that 'Hong Kong, no longer the trendsetter for popular culture in the Greater China area, has lost its ability to make popular cultural stars' (2013: 113). While Leung's career progression, like those of many of his contemporaries, owed much to Hong Kong's robust screen and celebrity cultures, newly emerging Chinese stars must position themselves within a much larger, if not more welcoming, media ecosystem. Mirana Szeto and Yun-Chung Chen lucidly describe mainlandisation as 'the tailoring of cultural content to what SARFT perceives as acceptable or not in mainland China' (2012: 120). While they stress that the term does not designate 'tailoring of content based on essentialist assumptions about cultural preferences and differences of Chinese audiences' (2012: 120), Hong Kong culture's mainlandisation parallels the contemporary phenomenon of Sinification (or Sinicisation), the spread of Han Chinese cultural influence. While Hong Kong's population is also overwhelmingly Han Chinese, its culture has historically been a hybrid one. Applied to Hong Kong, Sinification emphasises the fundamental Chineseness of ensuing cultural products, correspondingly limiting the ostensibly Western elements of Hong Kong's hybrid East/West culture. However useful such categorisations prove, Leung's most recent films show him distinctly pivoting toward the mainland in his choice of roles, if drawing on the same breadth of performance attributes he has developed across his career.

## Acting for the mainland

My approach here will be to frame Leung's late-2000s and early-2010s efforts broadly in terms of mainland cultural contexts, then to investigate the characters Leung plays and his particular performative inflections. The first task is relatively straightforward: all four films are explicitly nationalistic, partly indicating why only the two with action or martial-arts content, *Red Cliff* and *The Grandmaster*, secured measurable distribution outside East Asia. Even *The Grandmaster*, from longtime darling of global cinephile culture Wong Kar-Wai, hews so closely to present Communist Party and Chinese nationalist sentiments as to be largely indistinguishable from China's revived strand of domestic 'main melody' releases, those prosocial and avowedly 'healthy' films intended to 'invigorate national spirit and national pride' (Zhang 2008: 35).[5] The second task, scrutinising Leung's performances, poses other challenges: in *The Great Magician*, because of complicated plotting and the ensuing complexity with which his character's motivations are framed; in *The Silent War*, because he plays a totally blind character for most of the film, his face more minimally expressive than ever and his eyes obscured by dark glasses or opaque costume lenses; and in *Red Cliff* and *The Grandmaster*, because like name-brand co-stars Takeshi Kaneshiro in the former and Zhang Ziyi in the latter, he simply disappears from the films for long intervals.

Thus, we begin with the two-part epic *Red Cliff*, which adapts the fourteenth-century historical novel *The Romance of the Three Kingdoms*. Leung inherits a role originally planned for Chow Yun-Fat, though he had worked with director Woo in the past, first in the grim Vietnam War drama *Bullet in the Head* and then in the action film *Hard-Boiled*. *Red Cliff*'s scale and domestic success – Part I topped the Chinese box office in 2008, and Part II was the third-best performer in 2009 – kept Leung highly visible in the mainland context in particular.[6] *Red Cliff* again situates Leung, despite his top billing, in a supporting or co-starring role as the viceroy Zhou Yu, by turns a musician and a battlefield strategist. With the film's large ensemble cast and many elaborate army- and naval-battle set pieces, Leung is sidelined or entirely absent for large portions of the two-part film's nearly five-hour running time; he first appears over forty minutes into the first instalment. As in many previous films, his character embodies the film's philosophical and artistic core, though he dons armour as well for numerous action sequences (sometimes replaced with a stunt double). He also supplies much of its romantic content, as in an intimate scene with his wife, Xiao Qiao (Lin Chiling), in Part I that interrupts the wartime strategising and combat. The villain of the piece, General Cao Cao (Zhang Fengyi), also proclaims his desire to possess Xiao, granting Leung's Zhou a further stake in the overarching military conflict, particularly when in Part II Xiao ventures out alone to meet with Cao Cao to buy time for her side.

Leung shows off his equestrian skills in a battle scene in *Red Cliff* (2008)

As in the later *The Grandmaster*, Leung's role requires him (or the actor providing his Mandarin dubbing) to perform extensive monologues expounding on the film's themes (in this case, teamwork, strategy, brotherhood, loyalty and the like). Aside from flashes of expressiveness in battle scenes, he acts with the restraint that typifies his mature roles, though the film's limited characterisations render him something of a blank figure, not strongly psychologised at the narrative level. Nonetheless, in a scene of music performance alongside Kaneshiro's senior strategist Zhuge Liang, and in warmly lit bedroom scenes with Xiao, he displays soulfulness, warmth and attention to co-stars (or to the camera as proxy) that enable him to register as a substantive figure in the crowded, spectacle-dense film. He also reveals the most skin of anyone in the cast, twice appearing shirtless indoors, in amber lighting. Another brief indoor scene shows him balletically practising martial arts, a scene notable not just for Leung's graceful movements but also for his appearing alone, in contrast to the depiction of most principals exclusively in scenes with other characters.

In *Red Cliff*, Leung practises swordplay in a moment away from the large ensemble cast

Leung's performance, which receives considerably more screen time in Part II, does earn notice from critics in major US publications. In the *New York Times*'s review, Mike Hale (2009) calls Leung 'one of the world's last true matinee idols', and in the *Village Voice*, Scott Foundas (2009) offers a nearly identical judgment, naming Leung 'one of the last of the world's great movie stars'. Notably, neither reviewer qualifies his claim with reference to Leung's Chinese ethnicity. Meanwhile, Derek Elley argues in his *Variety* review that 'though not the most physically imposing thesp [sic] in the cast, Leung is easily the subtlest' (Elley 2008). Despite being surrounded with multiple large-scale and effects-heavy battle sequences, Leung's carefully modulated performance stands out enough to secure substantial international praise. With China figuring less prominently on the global political stage than it would just a few years later, reviewers approach Leung and the film more as entertainment vehicles than as carriers of ideology. Among Chinese viewerships, though, the very casting of Leung and others from outside mainland China can function as a political statement, as an implicit sign or affirmation of Chinese cultural unity. As Ruby Cheung argues, 'The diegetic call for Chinese national unification and unity in *Red Cliff* can also be found on a non-diegetic level via its cast, whose members come from different territories in East Asia' (Cheung 2016: 149). In this respect, *Red Cliff* in part echoes *Hero*, which also uses a polyglot cast (including mainlanders Jet Li and Zhang Ziyi, Hong Kong's Leung and Maggie Cheung, and the US-raised Donnie Yen) to interrogate, if not wholly endorse, Chinese nationalism.

In a different vein, we next move ahead two years to *The Great Magician*, which blends serious drama, intermittent action and outbursts of dry as well as near-slapstick humour. The film's dramatic elements involve political and military manoeuvring, and for Leung in particular, the unfulfilled romantic desire that defines many of his characters in prestige films since the 1990s. Continuing recent Chinese cinema's penchant for CGI-aided spectacles, the film also features multiple elaborate magic-show set pieces, mostly orchestrated by Leung, playing Zhang Xian, the film's titular prestidigitator. In accord with Chinese state prohibitions, though, the film shows him and a team of assistants planning most of the apparent feats of the supernatural, and late in the film his character delivers a speech cautioning against one of the state's longtime *bêtes noires*, superstition. The film is set in 1920s or 1930s Beijing,[7] with a coterie of Japanese villains and local warlords who collaborate with them. Leung's magician leads a team of proto-revolutionaries and seeks to reclaim his past lover, Yin (mainland star Zhou Xun), from the harem of the scheming warlord known as 'Bully Lei' (played by Lau Ching-Wan, veteran of more than 100 Hong Kong films and television series).[8] Though *Variety*'s Maggie Lee (2012) calls the film 'out of touch with contempo [sic] urban tastes',[9] numerous commentators attuned to local releases draw comparisons to the previous year's *Let the Bullets Fly* (2010), which for two years claimed the title of China's all-time box-office champion. Meanwhile, English-language reception includes repeated comparisons to US films *The Illusionist* (2006) and *The Prestige* (2006).

Based on a novel by Chinese author Zhang Haifan, and directed by Derek Yee (aka Yee Tung-Shing), previously known as director and producer of many contemporary Hong Kong crime thrillers, *The Great Magician* offers an array of stories and subplots, all in step with state values. Bully Lei makes a speech claiming his collaborations with the Japanese as purely instrumental, a temporary partnership in the service of Chinese power. In the film's final act, he teams up with magician Zhang to defeat this untrustworthy foreign presence. Female lead Yin leaves the film with her virtue unbesmirched, and betrothed to neither man. The film diverts Zhang's romantic longing for her into a plot to rescue her imprisoned father. Leung's performance shifts between what in Lee's judgment 'is initially rather wooden' – a possible consequence of playing the character as mysterious and with unstated motivations – and roundly charismatic. In his numerous stage-magic performances, and particularly in a party scene in which he flirtatiously conjures up jewellery for female guests, Leung exudes easy sexual charisma and bonhomie. At the same time, he makes a show of hiding emotions and motivations,

Leung charms party guests with magic tricks in *The Great Magician* (2011)

befitting both the magician's emphasis on maintaining enigmas and Zhang's need to conceal his revolutionary plan to kidnap Lei and free Yin's father.

Particularly in mainland releases that call for protagonists to behave in ways acceptable to SARFT censors, Leung's ability to suggest hidden motivations or contestatory sentiments is the key performative tool preventing his characters from serving as explicit vessels for blandly propagandistic sentiments.[10] Speaking in an interview about the film's period setting, Leung observes that 'troubled times always appeal to me more as they can be quite romantic and deplorably beautiful. Things can change by the second and you never know what's going to happen' (Wilkinson 2012). One can read his performance in terms of this productive uncertainty as well. Lin Yuting's review in Taiwan's *China Post* draws out the implications of this uncertainty: 'Because of the film's shifting stance, it is difficult to tell if its veiled commentary about the Chinese government ... is meant as literal endorsement or satiric criticism' (Lin 2012). As a period film and fantasy of sorts, *The Great Magician* may appear to stand at a remove from contemporary political concerns. Still, as Lin's review suggests, its complicated plotting, mutable character behaviours and thematisation of deception give Leung and his co-stars room to manoeuvre as performers, significant attractions amid China's expanding film industry and its authorities' inverse tolerance for dissent in popular entertainment.

Like many of Leung's films outside the realm of Hong Kong comedy-drama, *The Great Magician* calls for him to play a largely interiorised character in a resolutely exteriorised world. The film's emphasis on theatrical performance, and a subplot involving film production, call attention to the conditions of acting itself, to creating a persona for public consumption. Leung's next role, in the spy thriller and drama *The Silent War*, again shows him engaging in activities, and with technologies, that bridge private and public spheres. In this film – another adaptation, this time a 2006 novel from mainland writer Mai Jia[11] – set in the immediate aftermath of 1949's Communist revolution, he plays He Bing, a blind piano tuner recruited for a government counter-espionage programme. Many scenes feature Bing sitting among an array of shortwave radios, intercepting an anti-Communist cadre's Morse code messages. Once more, his character's motivations are contradictory or uncertain: he joins the group either for money or to ensure the safety of his mother, who appears threatened in a scene where he is first recruited. Later, his undeclared love for his handler, Zhang Xuening – again played by Zhou Xun – motivates him to work to exhaustion on the team's behalf. As in *The Great Magician*, his character in *The Silent War* diverts his romantic desire toward a goal benefiting the revolution.

*The Silent War* depicts a protagonist whose intimate engagement with a mass-media form benefits and cements his relationship with an explicit state, providing an allegory for stars such as Leung's own relation with the state-controlled Chinese film industry. Sabrina Qiong Yu, focusing on stars' vulnerability rather than power in the Chinese industry apparatus, notes that '"patriotism" … has become a basic criterion Chinese actors have to meet if they want to establish their stardom in the PRC', and that Hong Kong and Taiwan stars in particular must 'package themselves as patriotic stars in order to consolidate their star status and expand their fan base in the mainland' (Yu 2012b: 234, 235). *The Silent War* initially presents Bing as accomplice to a cad and (in US comic-book geek terms) a quasi-Daredevil figure, gifted with superhuman hearing in place of vision. Once under the wing of the sisterly Xuening, he quickly transforms into a tireless model worker. In numerous scenes, other characters remark on his toiling multiple days without sleep, possible in part because his residence is within the military complex where he and the scores of others we see work. Bing's fevered counter-surveillance stands for love of the nation on multiple levels. His labour serves an abstracted state battling a vague adversary; for most of the film, viewers receive little information about what 'the enemy' wants or seeks to subvert, apart from passing references to military secrets being

In *The Silent War* (2012), blind counter-spy Leung celebrates a prosocial victory

transmitted to the KMT. This labour also brings him explicitly into a community of pro-state worker/professionals, and ties him emotionally to Zhou's Xuening, with whom he can only connect in the work sphere. Though their onscreen chemistry, as in *The Great Magician*, is far from explosive, Leung and Zhou complement each other well as figures of unromance. Leung repeatedly plays men who long for women they cannot possess, and Zhou plays women who affectlessly ignore men's entreaties.[12] *The Silent War* thus channels facets of Leung's star persona from Hong Kong and transnational film – he who longs sexily and suffers virtuously – into the explicitly state-supporting mainland cinema.

Chinese stars do not operate within the same binary field of familiarity and unknowability that has long informed Hollywood's and other star systems. In their collection on Chinese film stars, Yingjin Zhang and Mary Farquhar note the designation after 1949 of stars as 'film workers', which sought 'to emphasize filmmaking as a collective social practice'. In this economy, star performance becomes 'a process of … self-moulding according to socialist templates of the model citizen in an idealized society' (Zhang and

Farquhar 2010: 9). More than six decades later, similar modelling still informed Chinese cinema and stardom. Articulating state policy on mainland films, SARFT party secretary Tian Jin observed in 2012 that 'Guidance is the soul' of mainland films, and that 'We always insist on political responsibility, social responsibility and cultural responsibility' (Johnson 2012). In this system, the responsibilities of film workers and film viewers intersect.

*The Silent War*, set in the immediate post-revolutionary moment, manipulates viewers' affect to combine the prescribed goals of stars, characters and audiences. At Xuening's urging, Bing undergoes an operation that restores his sight, but his newfound vision compromises his acute hearing ability. As he copes with this loss of prowess, Xuening sets out on an undercover mission to infiltrate the KMT spy ring, whose members brutally murder her. Bing then stabs out his own eyes so his heroic work can continue, and he wears a blindfold across his face for the film's final reels. The film therefore offers viewers first an aesthetically incomplete Leung, glasses or opaque lenses partly veiling his attractive eyes; then a whole one, his vision and full handsomeness restored; and finally a mutilated one, his features blocked further, and permanently.

Xiaoning Lu argues that Chinese cinema's designation of its stars as film workers 'helped re-conceptualize the relation between the star and the spectator: encouraging intimate camaraderie between the star and the spectator rather than spectators' craze for the star' (Lu 2010: 99). *The Silent War* explicitly positions its leads as part of a larger, prosocial group. Thus, the anonymous co-workers who assist Bing's radio surveillance offer proxies for audiences, encouraging viewers, for example, to share the emotions of the roomful of workers who cheer the team's finding of all 120 radio frequencies used by the enemy. Later, Bing's self-mutilation in service of state and its loveable, sacrificed representative Xuening provides another reminder of the contract into which viewers enter with the now mainlanded Leung, and the sacrifices of certain forms of viewing pleasure that new contract entails.

After his handler's murder in *The Silent War*, Leung reblinds himself to serve the Chinese state

This contract further entails the overwriting of the implicit relationship between films and audiences that prevailed in the much less regulated Hong Kong cinema of the pre-CEPA era. Stephen Teo claims that since the 1960s, 'Despite (or perhaps because of) its private nature, the Hong Kong film industry has actually sought to identify itself as a Chinese national cinema' but that 'the nationalism of [Shaw Brothers Studio] films and most Hong Kong films is abstract in heart and spirit' (2012: 286). With PRC backing and the content regulations on Hong Kong films' releases in the mainland market, layers of concrete nationalism now accompany those previously abstract sentiments. If the most recent work of iconoclastic Hong Kong filmmaker Wong Kar-Wai is any evidence, even those films and filmmakers invested in a cinema of artistry and emotion now pursue projects that appeal to mainland policy. Wong's *The Grandmaster* is, remarkably, the fifth screen treatment since 2008 of the biography and exploits of martial artist and national hero Ip Man (aka Yip Man; or in Mandarin, Ye Wen). Wong's version of the Ip Man story departs from that of the other films – Donnie Yen vehicles *Ip Man* (2008), *Ip Man 2* (2010) and the later *Ip Man 3* (2015), along with *The Legend Is Born: Ip Man* (2010) and *Ip Man: The Final Fight* (2013) – all of which mix *wuxia* and historical-drama genres though all too from Hong Kong directors best known for films with contemporary settings. *The Grandmaster* (its English title, with the Chinese title more accurately translatable either in the singular or plural) demonstrates Wong's continued interest in stories of Hong Kong's history, with archival film cut intermittently into the fictionalised story, which traverses the mid-1930s to the early 1950s. Filmed mostly in mainland studios rather than practical locations, though with Wong claiming to have travelled across China for pre-production interviews,[13] the finished film literally bridges the mainland and Hong Kong, with Leung's Ip Man eventually emigrating from Foshan in Guangdong (aka Canton) province to Hong Kong. While other contemporary film versions of the Ip Man story devote more time to his battles against the invading Japanese at the end of the 1930s, Wong's film emphasises the efforts of Ip Man and his allies to unify China's diverse martial-arts styles. It also gives weight to the unfulfilled romance between two of its 'grandmasters', Leung's Ip Man and Zhang Ziyi's Gong Er.

For numerous reasons, *The Grandmaster*'s performances thwart authoritative analysis: many of its stars saw their roles cut substantially in editing, and as for *The Silent War*, Leung's dialogue was redubbed by another actor for the Mandarin release.[14] Conversations as such between characters do not really occur; philosophical aphorisms dominate the spoken dialogue. Visually, principals often appear in slow motion even in conversation scenes, or in static poses, including many close-ups. This last feature gives some room for Leung's trademark facial expressiveness, which had been suppressed by costuming in *The Silent War*. However, his performance is something of a blank canvas, perhaps partly a consequence of the film's shooting over multiple years and its lack of a script, limiting actors' ability to show motivation. *Variety*'s

Maggie Lee (2013) finds that Leung 'lacks his usual intensity here [and that] his Ip Man reveals few distinct characteristics ... except humility', while in *Film Business Asia*, Derek Elley (2013) notes with frustration that Leung 'seems a lightweight in what should be his own movie' and that 'most of the time, he's more of a bystander to much richer, deeper personalities'. The bystander role, however, is a familiar one for Leung; as noted in Chapter 4, in many of his roles, he plays supporting or undemonstrative characters who embody films' sentimental or philosophical undercurrents. As such, his low-intensity performance in *The Grandmaster* allows him to stand equally, if undynamically, as a figure of romance, of martial-arts philosophy and of a Chinese patriotism that joins the mainland and Hong Kong.

The apparent blankness Leung presents in *The Grandmaster*, and similarly dampened affect or obscured psychology in *Red Cliff*, *The Great Magician* and *The Silent War*, offer viewers opportunities to read his performances as endorsements or critiques of the films' depictions of Chinese history and the socialist state. Leung's wide range of roles and acting styles across his career complicated efforts to locate him as a singular type. Perhaps ironically, his turn to more consistently interiorised performances in mainland films makes his characters and his overall star persona available for diverse responses.

# CONCLUSION

This short volume has sought to illuminate facets of Leung Chiu-Wai's acting and stardom that demonstrate not only the scope of his talent and his work's global circulation and acclaim, but also his status as a performer and cultural figure of great value to film and media scholars. Leung's career shows us how performers emerge in competitive creative economies such as Hong Kong's, how differing film cultures construct and receive creative agents such as stars, and how such agents can participate in (and be subjected to) critical discourse on film's political and social status. While I acknowledge that my lack of facility with Chinese-language primary evidence results in a negotiated treatment of information and discourse surrounding Leung, I hope my coverage here has been sufficiently thorough to indicate Leung's significance for English-language viewers and scholars as well as some of the cultural knowledge that Hong Kongers and other East Asian subjects use to apprehend his creative profile and output.

I conclude briefly with attention to Leung's present status as a major, mature star in Hong Kong and Chinese film industries as they continue their post-CEPA transformation and integration. As we have seen, a visible symptom of the mainlandisation of screen texts from greater China has been explicitly nationalistic, prosocial narratives. Cultural commentators have identified similar regional trends not driven by industrial shifts. Writing in *The Atlantic*, Patrick St Michel notes a rise in nationalist-themed films across East Asia's major film markets: 'Big patriotic movies are hardly unique to East Asia … but consumers in China, Korea, and Japan are embracing them against the backdrop of real-world geopolitical drama, and the demand for them has grown as diplomatic relations have worsened' (St Michel 2015). Nationalistic East Asian films may be a passing trend or a permanent sign of political influence. Whatever the case, as stars such as Leung work to maintain viable screen careers, they vividly reflect the accommodations and transformations of a Hong Kong cinema increasingly tied to its mainland counterpart. Hong Kong cinema's mainlandisation changes the terms on which its now co-produced films speak, addressing a mass East Asian audience only after navigating intermediate censorship. While screen performances are open texts that engender multifarious responses, mainlandisation can shift the inflections of screen workers' activity toward the official positions of the Chinese Communist Party, and away from the 'intention toward the Other' that Yiu-Wai Chu (2013: 162–3) identifies as a special characteristic of Hong Kong's culture.

Political concerns underlie the thematics and characterisations of Leung's recent mainland efforts, and perhaps also his preferred roles. In 2012, for example, motivated by personal preference or capitulation to state-enforced optimism, Leung publicly expressed a desire to play roles that were not 'depressing' or 'sad', telling *Beijing News*:

Sometimes, we as filmmakers have put too many depressing stories onto the silver screen. Now I don't want to bring so much sadness into my character and movies. … I've learned to look at things in life from [a] humorous angle and thus I would like to bring more happiness to the audience, too. Unfortunately, I can't find a proper script. (Chai 2012)

Politics also explicitly reshape Leung's ongoing career. He was confirmed in 2013 to star in the Japanese-Chinese co-production *1905*, to be the largest film to date from Japanese arthouse director

Kiyoshi Kurosawa. But with China–Japan tensions acutely escalating early in 2014 thanks to the territorial dispute over the Senkaku Islands (or as China calls them, the Diaoyu Islands), his involvement was jeopardised, and the project shut down, its Japanese production company bankrupted.[1] We might hope for Leung to appear in future regional co-productions that allow him to play a range of compelling characters, though China's fraught relations with many of its East Asian neighbours suggest that his near-term work will involve principally mainland cinema.[2] Still, the announcement in March 2016 that he would return to internationally inflected roles by starring in *Europe Raiders* (director Jingle Ma's follow-up to *Tokyo Raiders* and *Seoul Raiders*), with locations avowedly to include Italy, Austria and Japan alongside Shanghai, suggests that Leung hopes to maintain a presence in global film culture.[3]

Now in his mid-fifties, Leung continues to do screen acting that evidences his flexibility, mobility and durability. He most recently played the lead as a bar owner and romance guru in *See You Tomorrow* (aka *Bai du ren* or *The Ferryman*), a China/Hong Kong co-production from Alibaba Pictures, Mei Ah Entertainment and Wong Kar-Wai's Jet Tone Films, released at the end of 2016. The film is the directorial debut of hugely successful mainland short-story writer Zhang Jiajia (replacing Wong, who remains as producer), as well as the first screen adaptation of his work.[4] Also the first, high-profile release from the film arm of the Chinese e-commerce company Alibaba, *See You Tomorrow* adapts a story from Zhang's popular collection *I Belonged to You* (2013), which initially appeared on his much-trafficked Weibo microblog account as 'bedtime stories' in thirty-eight instalments in 2012 and 2013. Leung's casting suggests that film producers now regard him as a distinctive figure of mainland China's popular culture. (He co-stars for the fourth time alongside Takeshi Kaneshiro.) Before Leung's casting was announced, Mei Ah managing director Patrick Tong Hing-Chi identified the lead as a male star 'all women are crazy about'.[5] Tong's assertion brings us in many ways full circle, with sex appeal a prominent component of Leung's resilient screen stardom. Though his recent roles show him retreating from his longtime status as a global or transnational star, devotees of Leung's work may take solace in his ability to bring artistic depth, political and psychological complexity, and sensuous and other pleasures even to those roles that on many levels operate as conservative, state-flattering ideological guidance.

# NOTES

## Introduction

1   For Chinese names, film titles and occasional phrases, I use *pinyin* transliterations, mostly in Cantonese though sometimes in Mandarin instead, based on the most common usages in English-language discourse and on websites such as the Internet Movie Database. In contrast to IMDB style, I typically present Chinese actor and filmmaker names here with surname first, given name last (as with, for example, Wong Kar-Wai), though with exceptions when the people in question (for example, Tony Leung or John Woo) are known internationally by Anglicised names. As a general rule of thumb too, film and television characters' names appear in spellings supplied by English subtitles. As a non-Chinese speaker, I approach Leung's work at a disadvantage, but have periodically solicited the aid of native Cantonese and Mandarin speakers to lend nuance to claims about Leung and his media output.

## 1 How to act sexy

1   This charisma also accounts for the 'men want to be him, women want to sleep with him' appeal that popular critical discourse has identified with regard to his star persona. A *Newsweek* profile of Leung, for example, includes radio host Leung Tak-Man's assertion

that 'Girls like his style. Guys feel they grew up with him. He's just a regular guy' (quoted in Seno 2003). Likewise, *Giant Robot*'s Martin Wong and Eric Nakamura describe him as 'affable', saying to him, 'a lot of our female friends are totally in love with you' and then asking 'what can I do?' to emulate him (Wong and Nakamura 2001).

2  Regarding the perceived sex appeal and charisma of a Chinese star, Jet Li, known overwhelmingly for martial-arts rather than dramatic roles, see Yu (2010: 231).

3  See 'Tony Chiu Wai Leung: Awards', *IMDB Pro*, http://pro.imdb.com/name/nm0504897/awards, accessed 1 March 2015.

4  In regional circulation, and particularly in mainland China, film stars' often dubious cultural status bears mentioning. As Sabrina Qiong Yu observes, 'throughout Chinese film history, a star (in film or theatre) has usually had a poor reputation in the domain of morality' (2010: 234). Tang Wei faced an outcry about her lead role in *Lust, Caution* (both for her sex scenes and the political connotations of her character's affair with an anti-communist collaborator). China's SARFT regulatory board banned her from media appearances for two years, preventing her from working in mainland productions and resulting also in the withdrawal of her TV advertising work. For his part, Leung suffered no equivalent outcry or ban.

5  For an insightful reading of Leung's acting in these scenes and in other films, as well as a capsule biography, see Williams (2015).

6  *Lust, Caution*, budgeted at $15 million, earned over million in theatrical release, including over $17 million (or over 31 per cent of its total gross) in mainland China. It earned large receipts in South Korea, Hong Kong and Taiwan too, with higher box-office totals in each of those than in the US or any European country.

7  The box-office data site Box Office Mojo does not list global grosses for *Chungking Express*, but it does show a North American gross for the film of only $600,200, presumably well below its receipts in Hong Kong or elsewhere in the region. See 'Chungking Express', *Box Office Mojo*, http://boxofficemojo.com/movies/?id=chungkingexpress.htm, accessed 22 March 2015.

8   As Lo argues, in a range of 1980s and 1990s Hong Kong films, 'localism no longer pertains to the culture and customs of a particular place' but appears 'in relation to other cultures and other localities' (2005: 113–14).

9   The Internet Movie Database lists *Lust, Caution* as a US/China/ Taiwan co-production and includes one Hong Kong company among its co-producers. While set entirely in China, it includes location filming not only in China but also in Hong Kong and Malaysia. US stakeholders include writer-producer James Schamus, his affiliated producer-distributor Focus Features and director Ang Lee, Taiwan-born but US-based since the late 1970s. For *Lust, Caution*'s company and other credits, see 'Lust, Caution', *IMDB Pro*, https://pro-labs.imdb.com/title/tt0808357/, accessed 22 March 2015.

10  Interviewing editor Patrick Tam, Stephen Teo reports that 'originally the scene was to play like a trailer announcing Tony Leung Chiu-wai as the star of the next episode' (Teo 2005: 45).

11  For a detailed formal analysis of the final scenes, see Bordwell (2008).

12  Less racily, Leung and Cheung grapple on a bed again later in the film, fully clothed, and later still Leung receives oral sex from a stranger in a movie theatre.

13  Stephen Teo (2005: 105–9) provides a detailed reading of *Happy Together*'s gender dynamic, both supporting and refuting the idea of Lai and Ho as a couple occupying connotative husband (Lai) and wife (Ho) roles.

14  Still, Leung had earlier named the role his personal favourite. As he recounts in *Buenos Aires Zero Degree: The Making of Happy Together* (1999):

It's been some time since I was satisfied by a role. People ask which role I'm most pleased with. I always say *Days of Being Wild*, even though I was in only one shot. Ask me which role I'm most pleased with now, and I'll say *Happy Together*.

Leung may spin his claim for the benefit of the making-of documentary's subject, but his celebration of the work Wong 'pushed' him to do remains noteworthy.

15  I use the term 'persona' periodically across this book, though as Leung
    Wing-Fai (2015: 59) notes, it has no precise equivalent in Cantonese,
    with the term *xingxiang*, or 'image', the standard substitute.

16  While Chow is seven years older than Leung and began appearing in
    film and television in the mid-1970s, the two actors' careers intersected
    repeatedly in the 1980s and early 1990s, in four mid-1980s TVB series
    and as co-stars in a trio of films.

17  For surveys of Chinese constructions of the body, see for example
    Heinrich and Martin (2006) and Zito and Barlow (1994).

## 2 1980s Hong Kong television and early film efforts

1  The 1986 series also appears in English translations as *New Heavenly
   Sword and Dragon Sabre* or as *The Heaven Sword and Dragon Saber*.
   Throughout this chapter, I try to give the most commonly used English
   translations of series titles as they appear on home-video releases or in
   listings of websites such as the Internet Movie Database (www.imdb.
   com), Hong Kong Cinemagic (www.hkcinemagic.com) and the Hong
   Kong Movie Database (www.hkmdb.com).

2  See Lo (2011).

3  For *Soldier of Fortune* airdates, see 'Soldier of Fortune', *DramaWiki*,
   http://wiki.d-addicts.com/Soldier_of_Fortune and '*Soldier of Fortune*
   (1982 TV Series)', *Wikipedia*, http://en.wikipedia.org/wiki/Soldier_of_
   Fortune_(1982_TV_series), both accessed 11 January 2016.

4  For *The Duke of Mount Deer* airdates, see '*The Duke of Mount Deer*
   (1984 TV Series)', *Wikipedia*, shttp://en.wikipedia.org/wiki/The_Duke_
   of_Mount_Deer_(1984_TV_series), accessed 11 January 2016.

5  TVB's 'Five Tigers' include Leung, Lau, Michael Mui, Kent Tong
   and Felix Wong. On this group, see 'Five Tiger Generals', *Wikipedia*,
   http://en.wikipedia.org/wiki/Five_Tiger_Generals_of_TVB, accessed
   11 January 2016.

6  For *The Grand Canal* airdates, see 'The Grand Canal', *DramaWiki*,
   http://wiki.d-addicts.com/The_Grand_Canal, accessed 11 January 2016.

7   English translation from an essay by Leung in *Hong Kong Screen Idol* (December 1983).

8   For TVB 1983 series information, see 'List of TVB Series (1983)', *Wikipedia*, http://en.wikipedia.org/wiki/List_of_TVB_series_(1983), accessed 11 January 2016.

9   For plot summary of *The Clones* (out of print in its DVD edition), see 'The Clones', *YesAsia.com*, http://www.yesasia.com/us/the-clones-dv d-end-tvb-drama-us-version/1011875787-0-0-0-en/info.html, accessed 7 January 2016.

10  For TVB 1984 series information, see 'List of TVB Series (1984)', *Wikipedia*, http://en.wikipedia.org/wiki/List_of_TVB_series_(1984), accessed 11 January 2016.

11  Leung Wing-Fai here quotes TVB alumnus Kam Kwok-leung, who remarks, 'The training class was very comprehensive and we learned acting theory, music, make-up, martial arts, the art of attack and defence, dance, etc.' (Hong Kong International Film Festival 1999: 135; Leung's translation).

12  See Naremore (1988) esp. pp. 28–30.

13  James Naremore defines the idiolect as 'a set of performing traits that is systematically highlighted in films' (1988: 4).

14  See Curtin (2007: 111–12).

15  On TVB's overseas rental outlets, see Curtin (2003: 219 and 2007: 112) as well as Kong (2008: 35).

16  As Curtin observes, 'TVB series about ancient dynasties and kung fu heroes tended to attract ethnic Chinese viewers in Southeast Asia, but dubbed versions also performed well among Malay, Thai, Cambodian, Vietnamese, Korean and Japanese audiences' (2007: 112). See also Ma (1999: 39–40), who notes TVB's overseas expansion beginning in the early 1980s and the rise of VCRs in the late 1980s (the latter contributing to TVB's overseas video-rental market).

17  Home-video formats offer another index of TVB series' circulation and prospective audiences. As of 2015, many *wuxia* series featuring Leung – *The Duke of Mount Deer*, *The Yang's Saga* and *The New Heaven Sword and Dragon Sabre* – were available in English-subtitled DVD editions. *Angels and Devils*, the fantastic *The Superpower* and some other

series also appear on DVD, though not in English-subtitled editions. Meanwhile, the three *Police Cadet* series remain available, but only in Chinese-language VCD editions. TVB's home-video division thus regards *Police Cadet* as chiefly of interest to Chinese-speaking viewers.

18  In another *Hong Kong Screen Idol* essay, Leung writes:

Recently, I declined several movie offers. Friends think it's rather foolish of me not to cash in the opportunities. ... I agree money is important to a degree. But, health is vital too. ... I am telling you today, a few million dollars does not mean a thing to me. ... Health is my top priority. Money comes in second or third. ('1983–1986: HK Screen Idols Tony Leung' n.d.; English translation from an essay by Leung in *Hong Kong Screen Idol* [October 1985]).

19  Inconsistent cataloguing of release dates for Hong Kong films in English-language resources makes it difficult to specify Leung's output. The Internet Movie Database lists only six 1993 releases starring Leung, but IMDB has extensive gaps in coverage of East Asian film and television. The Hong Kong Movie Database shows nine 1993 releases with Leung, while Hong Kong Cinemagic and the fan site tonyleung.info both list ten 1993 releases for Leung. All told, the three databases show Leung starring in between twenty-six and twenty-eight films from 1991 to 1995.

20  Wimal Dissanayake (2003: 1) notes that *Ashes of Time*'s production stretched over two years, during which time Wong also filmed *Chungking Express* and executive-produced *The Eagle-Shooting Heroes*, both co-starring Leung.

21  Lau co-stars in the film too, with a role granting her much more screen time than Leung.

22  Multiple sources, including IMDB, incorrectly assert Leung's first film as the 1982 Chuck Norris vehicle *Forced Vengeance*. The more authoritative Academy of Motion Picture Arts and Sciences (AMPAS) database identifies the other Tony Leung, Leung Ka-Fai, as the actual actor in the small part in question. See AMPAS (n.d.).

23  I do not mean to imply that homosexuality requires 'soft' representations, only that Leung has played his gay roles on such terms.

24 Leung Wing-Fai offers extensive, insightful work on Lau, including analysis of his music career and performances (see Leung 2015: 97–103). With more than sixty albums to his credit, Lau is a much more prolific and successful singer than Leung, though music remains a notable facet of Leung's own multimedia stardom, particularly within Hong Kong.

25 Here as elsewhere, I am indebted to the comprehensive fan site tonyleung.info, which lists many of Leung's CD releases, features many songs and song clips, and provides original Chinese lyrics. See 'Tony's Music Album' (n.d.) and related pages on the site.

## 3 Pan-Asian and global at-cinema stardom

1 In theatrical release, *In the Mood for Love* played at its peak on seventy-four screens in the US, grossing nearly $3 million (as part of a global total of nearly $13 million), all significant numbers for a non-action East Asian release. See 'In the Mood for Love', *Box Office Mojo*, http://www.boxofficemojo.com/movies/?id=inthemoodforlove.htm, accessed 3 November 2015.

2 Shelly Kraicer (2005) makes a similar point, specifically in regard to films from director Wong Kar-Wai; he also notes the multitude of genres that comprise commercial Hong Kong cinema. Still, the dominance of popular genres in Hong Kong film culture means that many dramatic works qualify by default as arthouse products. For example, a *South China Morning Post* preview of a 2013 screening of 1986's *Love Unto Waste* is titled 'Art House: Love Unto Waste' (Lee 2013). A deep but scarcely modernist drama, the film has a festival-approved director, Stanley Kwan, though also casts Leung and Chow Yun-Fat, both major stars migrating in the 1980s from popular TVB series.

3 Cotillard played the lead female role in the first three *Taxi* films, with the third released in 2003.

4 For example, an IMDB user review of the TVB series *The Duke of Mount Deer* features the title 'Tony Leung like You've Never Seen Him' (J_Charles 2005).

5  Steve Neale understands national language in art films as 'a mark which serves simultaneously as a sign of their cultural status and a sign of their national origin' (1981: 35). In this formulation, any foreign-language release would acquire the cultural status of art film.

6  Cases exist where such juxtapositions offer novelty value, as with the de facto stunt casting of Adam Sandler in *Punch-Drunk Love* (2002) or Jean-Claude Van Damme in *JCVD* (2008), though these works arguably do not deterritorialise their stars the way international festivals do for stars with largely national or regional reputations.

7  While I have read many seemingly credible accounts of on-set activity, such accounts often cannot be verified, making them less than ideal primary resources, contestable and probably incomplete. I draw on them only occasionally, partly because of the evidentiary caveats facing researchers.

8  Box Office Mojo reports the film's worldwide theatrical gross as just over $64 million, led by $45 million in receipts in China, and with only $6 million in North America ('The Grandmaster', *Box Office Mojo*, http://www.boxofficemojo.com/movies/?page=main&id=grandmasters.htm, accessed 7 January 2016).

9  Reviewers such as Therese Lacson (2013) report on the different language versions and the curiously multilingual US release.

10  Thanks also to the anonymous reviewer of this manuscript who suggested glossing the implications of Leung's silent performance.

11  David Bordwell analyses *Chungking Express*'s style in his *Planet Hong Kong*, identifying what he terms 'biplanar rates of motion' in this shot and others (2000: 288).

# 4 Tony Leung and genre stardom

1  On *Hero*'s complex politics and its interrogation of Chinese nationalism, see essays in Rawnsley and Rawnsley (2010), particularly editor Gary D. Rawnsley's own 'The Political Narrative(s) of *Hero*'.

2  The 'Asian Clark Gable' reference appears repeatedly, variantly attributed to a French newspaper, to actor Robert De Niro and even to Leung himself in relation to the moustache of his character in *2046*.

3 See 'Red Cliff', *Box Office Mojo*, http://www.boxofficemojo.com/movies/?id=redcliff.htm, accessed 23 November 2015.

4 See Gallagher (2015) for a more extensive treatment of East Asian film-noir discourse and Leung's framing as a noir figure.

5 For example, touching on noir themes of unarticulated social anxiety, Gina Marchetti reads Leung's character in *Chungking Express* in terms of the then-approaching 1997 return to Chinese governance: 'Cop 663 may be thinking of the future when he turns in his colonial police uniform to run a carryout' (2006: 36).

6 For more on the films' local impact, see Rayns (2004), Marchetti (2007) and Leung (2008).

7 See 'Lust, Caution', *Box Office Mojo*, http://boxofficemojo.com/movies/?id=lustcaution.htm, accessed 11 December 2015.

8 After *Hero* too, *Lust, Caution* (a co-production among companies in the US, China, Taiwan and Hong Kong) stands as Leung's most commercially successful film outside East Asia, its global box-office returns in excess of $67 million narrowly outpacing *The Grandmaster*'s $64 million. As verifiable statistics for non-US productions are difficult to obtain, no reliable data exists for the global theatrical grosses of Hong Kong and Chinese productions such as *Infernal Affairs* and *Red Cliff*. The first instalment of *Red Cliff* broke Chinese box-office records in summer 2008 but performed modestly in piecemeal international distribution.

# 5 The mainlanding of Tony Leung Chiu-Wai

1 For more about CEPA, see 'Mainland and Hong Kong Closer Economic Partnership Arrangement (CEPA)' (2012).

2 During the interval between the releases of the two parts of *Red Cliff*, Leung also appeared in the limited international release of *Ashes of Time Redux* (2008), the recut version of 1994's *Ashes of Time*.

3 See 'The Grandmaster', *Box Office Mojo*, n.d. http://www.boxofficemojo.com/movies/?page=main&id=grandmasters.htm, accessed 16 December 2015.

4 The Internet Movie Database shows *Lust, Caution*'s filming locations in China, Hong Kong and Malaysia, *Red Cliff*'s in China and Taiwan,

and *The Silent War* with exclusively mainland shooting. IMDB does not provide location information for *The Great Magician* or comprehensive data for *The Grandmaster*, though credits note crews in Hong Kong and Japan for the former and in Hong Kong and China for the latter.

5   For a succinct glossing of the 2000s resurgence of main-melody releases, see Sun (2010).

6   The two parts debuted in June 2008 and January 2009, respectively. On *Red Cliff*'s performance in China, see *Box Office Mojo*'s annual summaries at http://www.boxofficemojo.com/intl/china/yearly/?yr=2008 and http://www.boxofficemojo.com/intl/china/yearly/?yr=2009, both accessed 24 December 2015.

7   Most English-language reviews note a 1920s setting, though *Time Out*'s Beijing edition gives the time period as the 1930s, even quoting Leung to that effect, one quote beginning 'I don't know much about 1930s Beijing' (Wilkinson 2012). A 1920s period seems plausible given a subplot involving production of a silent film; China's first sound film appeared in 1930.

8   At the end of 2011, Leung also appeared in a video teaser (initially available at https://www.youtube.com/watch?v=0dFdNrwm2B0 but eventually deleted) for a short film directed by Zhou, *Five Demon Traps*, set for 2012 release, though the film in question has yet to appear.

9   'Out of touch' or not, the film did well in Chinese release, grossing over $27 million (nearly RMB 174 million) and standing as the top domestic release in the first half of 2012 (though slipping to the number-nine domestic release by year-end, with *The Silent War* placing sixth overall). See 'China Box Office up 37% in First Half of 2012' (2012), 'List of Chinese Films of 2012' (2013) and Sun (2013).

10   SARFT, the State Administration of Radio, Film and Television, was the title of China's media-censorship body through 2013. Now taking on print censorship as well, it has since been renamed SAPPRFT (the State Administration of Press, Publication, Radio, Film and Television).

11   Noted in Elley (2012).

12   On Zhou's persona, see Shin (2015). In *The Silent War*, Leung's character marries a different co-worker, and Zhou's thinks intimate thoughts about her sometime boss, Devil (Wang Xuebing), so a romance between the two leads does not develop.

13  Wong observes in an interview that 'I spent three years on the road. Starting from Beijing I went from town to town to interview hundreds of masters' (Lim 2013).

14  With both films, Mandarin redubbing causes unhappiness. Derek Elley's review (2012) of *The Silent War* judges that Leung has been 'given a totally unsuitable voice in his Mandarin redubbing', and regarding *The Grandmaster*, Leung himself notes that on viewing the Mandarin version, 'I felt like "dying" upon hearing the dubbed voice. Wong Kar Wai wanted me to dub my voice but there is no time' ('Tony Leung Almost "Dies" after Hearing His Voice Dubbing' 2013).

# Conclusion

1  The film's Wikipedia entry at http://en.wikipedia.org/wiki/1905_(film) (accessed 17 December 2015) outlines the production's history and cessation; see also 'Film Company Prenom H Goes Bankrupt' (2013).

2  News in July 2015 of Donnie Yen's casting in a *Star Wars* sequel mentioned a number of other Chinese stars under consideration for the (apparently ethnically specific) role, including Stephen Chow, Jet Li and notably, Leung himself. Though the news emerged from China's not always reliable *Apple Daily*, if accurate, it suggests that despite past claims of uninterest in Hollywood work, Leung was pursuing such activity, if quietly or at the behest of his agent, WME's Elyse Scherz. See 'Action Star Donnie Yen Clinches Jedi Role in Episode VIII of Star Wars' (2015).

3  See Chu (2016) for news of the announced production.

4  See Ma (2015).

5  See Fischer (2014), citing Hong Kong newspaper *The Standard* as the source of Tong's statement.

# BIBLIOGRAPHY

'Action Star Donnie Yen Clinches Jedi Role in Episode VIII of Star Wars',
*Straits Times* (Singapore), 6 July 2015, http://www.straitstimes.com/
lifestyle/entertainment/action-star-donnie-yen-clinches-jedi-role-
in-episode-viii-of-star-wars, accessed 28 December 2015.

AMPAS, 'Index to Motion Picture Credits: Forced Vengeance',
*Oscars.org*, n.d., http://wwwdb.oscars.org:8100/servlet/impc.
DisplayCredits?primekey_in=1999090818:55:4025-167175, accessed
27 October 2015.

Baron, Cynthia, 'Suiting Up for Postmodern Performance in John Woo's
*The Killer*', in Cynthia Baron, Diane Carson and Frank P. Tomasulo
(eds), *More than a Method: Trends and Traditions in Contemporary
Film Performance* (Detroit, MI: Wayne State University Press, 2004),
pp. 297–330.

Baron, Cynthia and Sharon Marie Carnicke, *Reframing Screen Performance*
(Ann Arbor: University of Michigan Press, 2008).

Berry, Chris, 'Stellar Transit: Bruce Lee's Body or Chinese Masculinity
in a Transnational Frame', in Larissa Heinrich and Fran Martin (eds),
*Embodied Modernities: Corporeality, Representation and Chinese Cultures*
(Honolulu: University of Hawaii Press, 2006), pp. 218–34.

Bettinson, Gary, *The Sensuous Cinema of Wong Kar-Wai: Film Poetics and
the Aesthetics of Disappearance* (Hong Kong: Hong Kong University
Press, 2015).

Bordo, Susan, *The Male Body: A New Look at Men in Public and in Private*
(New York: Farrar, Straus and Giroux, 2000).

Bordwell, David, 'The Art Cinema as a Mode of Film Practice', in Marshall Cohen and Leo Braudy (eds), *Film Theory and Criticism: Introductory Readings*, 5th edn (New York: Oxford University Press, 1999 [1979]), pp. 716–24.

Bordwell, David, *Planet Hong Kong: Popular Cinema and the Art of Entertainment* (Madison: University of Wisconsin Press, 2000).

Bordwell, David, 'Years of Being Obscure', *davidbordwell.net*, June 2008, http://www.davidbordwell.net/blog/2008/06/, accessed 25 September 2015.

Bruzzi, Stella, *Undressing Cinema: Clothing and Identity in the Movies* (London: Routledge, 1997).

Chai, Peter, 'Tony Leung's Psychological Challenge', *Yahoo! Entertainment Singapore*, 7 January 2012, http://sg.entertainment.yahoo.com/news/tony-leungs-psychological-challenge-031612855.html, accessed 10 June 2013.

Chan, Joseph M. and Anthony Y.-H. Fung, 'Structural Hybridization in Film and Television Production in Hong Kong', in Kwok-bun Chan (ed.), *Hybrid Hong Kong* (London: Routledge, 2013), pp. 108–20.

Chang, Eileen, Wang Hui Ling and James Schamus, *Lust, Caution: The Story, the Screenplay, and the Making of the Film* (New York: Pantheon Books, 2007).

Cheung, Ruby, *New Hong Kong Cinema: Transitions to Becoming Chinese in 21st-Century East Asia* (New York: Berghahn Books, 2016).

'China Box Office up 37% in First Half of 2012', *Screen Daily*, 6 July 2012, http://www.screendaily.com/news/asia-pacific/china-box-office-up-37-in-first-half-of-2012/5044150.article, accessed 10 June 2013.

Chow, Rey, *The Protestant Ethnic and the Spirit of Capitalism* (New York: Columbia University Press, 2002).

Chu, Karen, 'Filmart: Jet Tone Unveils "Europe Raiders"', *Hollywood Reporter*, 13 March 2016, http://www.hollywoodreporter.com/news/filmart-jet-tone-unveils-europe-874958, accessed 7 June 2016.

Chu, Yiu-Wai, *Lost in Transition: Hong Kong Culture in the Age of China* (Ithaca: State University of New York Press, 2013).

Curtin, Michael, 'Media Capital: Towards the Study of Spatial Flows', *International Journal of Cultural Studies* vol. 6 no. 2 (2003), pp. 202–28.

Curtin, Michael, *Playing to the World's Biggest Audience: The Globalization of Chinese Film and Television* (Berkeley: University of California Press, 2007).

Dargis, Manohla, 'A Cad and a Femme Fatale Simmer' (film review), *New York Times*, 28 September 2007, http://www.nytimes.com/2007/09/28/movies/28lust.html, accessed 23 November 2015.

Dissanayake, Wimal with Dorothy Wong, *Ashes of Time* (Hong Kong: Hong Kong University Press, 2003).

Doyle, Christopher, *Buenos Aires* (Tokyo: Prénom H, 1997).

Doyle, Christopher, 'Don't Try for Me, Argentina' in John Boorman and Walter Donohue (eds), *Projections 8: Film-makers on Film-making* (London: Faber & Faber, 1998), pp. 154–82. Reprinted at http://www.tonyleung.info/goodies/chris.shtml, accessed 10 June 2016.

Elley, Derek, 'Flowers of Shanghai' (film review), *Variety*, 20 May 1998, http://variety.com/1998/film/reviews/flowers-of-shanghai-1117477540/, accessed 17 November 2015.

Elley, Derek, 'Red Cliff' (film review), *Variety*, 20 July 2008, http://variety.com/2008/film/markets-festivals/red-cliff-1200508249/, accessed 28 December 2015.

Elley, Derek, 'The Silent War' (film review), *Film Business Asia*, 29 August 2012, http://www.filmbiz.asia/reviews/the-silent-war, accessed 9 June 2013.

Elley, Derek, 'The Grandmaster' (film review), *Film Business Asia*, 28 January 2013, http://www.filmbiz.asia/reviews/the-grandmaster, accessed 9 June 2013.

Farquhar, Mary and Yingjin Zhang (eds), *Chinese Film Stars* (London: Routledge).

Feng, Lin, *Chow Yun-Fat and Territories of Hong Kong Stardom* (Edinburgh: Edinburgh University Press, 2017).

'Film Company Prenom H Goes Bankrupt – Tony Leung's Involvement Cancelled Due to Senkaku Dispute', *MSN Sankei News Japan: The Sankei Shimbun & Sankei Digital*, 25 February 2013, http://sankei.jp.msn.com/entertainments/news/130225/ent13022512470019-n1.htm, accessed 29 December 2015.

Fischer, Russ, 'Wong Kar-Wai Prepping a New Movie to Shoot in 2015', /Film, 20 June 2014, http://www.slashfilm.com/wong-kar-wai-film-2015/, accessed 17 December 2015.

Foundas, Scott, 'John Woo's Killer Instincts Return for *Red Cliff*' (film review), *Village Voice*, 17 November 2009, http://www.villagevoice.com/film/john-woos-killer-instincts-return-for-red-cliff-6392183, accessed 28 December 2015.

Gallagher, Mark, '"Would You Rather Spend More Time Making Serious Cinema?": *Hero* and Tony Leung's Polysemic Masculinity', in Gary D. Rawnsley and Ming-Yeh T. Rawnsley (eds), *Global Chinese Cinema: The Culture and Politics of Hero* (London: Routledge, 2010), pp. 106–20.

Gallagher, Mark, 'Tony Leung's Thrillers and Transnational Stardom', in Chi-Yun Shin and Mark Gallagher (eds), *East Asian Film Noir* (London: I. B. Tauris, 2015), pp. 197–214.

Hale, Mike, 'It's Good Guys vs. Bad Guys on a China-Size Scale' (film review), *New York Times*, 17 November 2009, http://www.nytimes.com/2009/11/18/movies/18redcliff.html, accessed 28 December 2015.

Hay, John, 'The Body Invisible in Chinese Art?', in Angela Zito and Tani E. Barlow (eds), *Body, Subject, and Power in China* (Chicago: University of Chicago Press, 1994), pp. 42–77.

Heinrich, Ari Larissa, *The Afterlife of Images: Translating the Pathological Body between China and the West* (Durham, NC: Duke University Press, 2008).

Heinrich, Larissa and Fran Martin (eds), *Embodied Modernities: Corporeality, Representation and Chinese Cultures* (Honolulu: University of Hawaii Press, 2006).

Hodges, Graham Russell Gao, *Anna May Wong: From Laundryman's Daughter to Hollywood Legend* (Basingstoke: Palgrave Macmillan, 2012 [2004]).

Hong Kong International Film Festival *Hong Kong New Wave – Twenty Years After* (Hong Kong: HKIFF, 1999).

Hoskins, Colin and Rolf Mirus, 'Reasons for the US Dominance of the International Trade in Television Programmes', *Media, Culture and Society* vol. 10 no. 4 (October 1988), pp. 499–515.

Hu, Brian, 'The KTV Aesthetic: Popular Music Culture and Contemporary Hong Kong Cinema', *Screen* vol. 47 no. 4 (Winter 2006), pp. 407–24.

'1983–1986: HK Screen Idols Tony Leung', *Hong Kong Screen Idol*, n.d. Reprinted at http://tonyleung.info/tony/?p=897, accessed 11 January 2016.

'Interview with Tony Leung', *Hong Kong Panorama 2000–2001* (Hong Kong: HKIFF, 2001). Reprinted at http://tonyleung.info/news/hkpanorama1.shtml, accessed 10 December 2015.

J_Charles, 'Reviews & Ratings for "Luk ding gei"', *Internet Movie Database*, 29 July 2005, http://www.imdb.com/title/tt0449734/reviews, accessed 7 June 2014.

Johnson, Ian, 'China, at Party Congress, Lauds Its Cultural Advances', *New York Times*, 12 November 2012, http://www.nytimes.com/2012/11/12/world/asia/china-at-party-congress-touts-its-cultural-advances.html, accessed 12 November 2012.

Kar, Law, 'An Overview of Hong Kong's New Wave Cinema', in Esther C. M. Yau (ed.), *At Full Speed: Hong Kong Cinema in a Borderless World* (Minneapolis: University of Minnesota Press, 2001), pp. 31–52.

Ko, Claudine, 'Mr. Wong Kar-Wai', *Giant Robot* vol. 21 (2001), pp. 37–9.

Kong, Lily, 'Shaw Cinema Enterprise and Understanding Cultural Industries', in Poshek Fu (ed.), *China Forever: The Shaw Brothers and Diasporic Cinema* (Urbana: University of Illinois Press, 2008), pp. 27–56.

Kovács, András Bálint , *Screening Modernism: European Art Cinema, 1950–1980* (Chicago, IL: University of Chicago Press, 2007).

Kraicer, Shelly, 'Tracking the Elusive Wong Kar-Wai' (book review), *Cineaste* vol. 30 no. 4 (Fall 2005), pp. 14–15.

Lacson, Therese, 'The Grandmaster Is Beautiful, but Flawed' (film review), *Nerdophiles: A Collective Blog on Nerd Culture*, 31 August 2013, http://www.nerdophiles.com/2013/08/31/the-grandmaster-is-beautiful-but-flawed/, accessed 11 November 2015.

Lee, Edmund, 'Art House: Love Unto Waste' (film review), *South China Morning Post* (*48 Hours* magazine supplement), 11 July 2013, http://www.scmp.com/magazines/48hrs/article/1276070/art-house-love-unto-waste, accessed 10 June 2014.

Lee, Maggie, 'The Great Magician' (film review), *Variety*, 11 January 2012, http://www.variety.com/VE1117946820, accessed 17 November 2012.

Lee, Maggie, 'The Grandmaster' (film review), *Variety*, 8 January 2013, http://www.variety.com/2013/film/reviews/the-grandmaster-1117948960/, accessed 9 June 2013.

Lee, Vivian P. Y., *Hong Kong Cinema since 1997: The Post-Nostalgic Imagination* (Basingstoke: Palgrave Macmillan, 2009).

Leung, Wing-Fai, '*Infernal Affairs* and *Kung Fu Hustle*: Panacea, Placebo and Hong Kong Cinema', in Leon Hunt and Leung Wing-Fai (eds), *East Asian Cinemas: Exploring Transnational Connections on Film* (London: I. B. Tauris, 2008), pp. 71–87.

Leung, Wing-Fai, *Multimedia Stardom in Hong Kong: Image, Performance and Identity* (London: Routledge, 2015).

Leung, Wing-Fai and Andy Willis (eds), *East Asian Film Stars* (Basingstoke: Palgrave Macmillan, 2014).

Lim, Dennis, 'Berlin Film Festival: Wong Kar-wai, Kung Fu Auteur', *New York Times*, 16 February 2013, http://artsbeat.blogs.nytimes.com/2013/02/16/berlin-film-festival-wong-kar-wai-kung-fu-auteur/, accessed 9 June 2013.

Lin, Yuting, 'The Great Magician' (film review), *China Post*, 3 February 2012, http://www.chinapost.com.tw/movie/comedy/2012/02/03/330529/The-Great.htm, accessed 10 June 2013.

'List of Chinese Films of 2012', *Wikipedia*, 16 May 2013, http://en.wikipedia.org/wiki/Chinese_films_of_2012, accessed 10 June 2013.

Lo, Alex, 'A Golden Age when TVB Dictated Popular Culture', *South China Morning Post*, 28 January 2011, http://www.scmp.com/article/736941/golden-age-when-tvb-dictated-popular-culture, accessed 23 October 2015.

Lo, Kwai-Cheung, *Chinese Face/Off: The Transnational Popular Culture of Hong Kong* (Urbana: University of Illinois Press, 2005).

Louie, Kam, *Theorising Chinese Masculinity: Society and Gender in China* (Cambridge: Cambridge University Press, 2002).

Louie, Kam and Louise Edwards, 'Chinese Masculinity: Theorizing Wen and Wu', *East Asian History* vol. 8 (1994), pp. 135–48.

Lu, Xiaoning, 'Zhang Ruifang: Modelling the Socialist Red Star', in Yinglin Zhang and Mary Farquhar (eds), *Chinese Film Stars* (London: Routledge, 2010), pp. 97–107.

Ma, Eric Kit-wai, *Culture, Politics and Television in Hong Kong* (London: Routledge, 1999).

Ma, Kevin, 'Alibaba Teams with Wong Kar-Wai on Ferryman', *Film Business Asia*, 18 January 2015, http://www.filmbiz.asia/news/alibaba-teams-with-wong-kar-wai-on-ferryman, accessed 17 December 2015.

'Mainland and Hong Kong Closer Economic Partnership Arrangement (CEPA)', Trade and Industry Department, The Government of the Hong Kong Special Administrative Region, 2012, http://www.tid.gov.hk/english/cepa/, accessed 7 January 2016.

Marchetti, Gina, *Romance and the 'Yellow Peril': Race, Sex and Discursive Strategies in Hollywood Fiction* (Berkeley: University of California Press, 1993).

Marchetti, Gina, *From Tian'anmen to Times Square: Transnational China and the Chinese Diaspora on Global Screens, 1989–1997* (Philadelphia Temple University Press, 2006).

Marchetti, Gina, *Andrew Lau and Alan Mak's Infernal Affairs – The Trilogy* (Hong Kong: Hong Kong University Press, 2007).

Maunder, Trish, 'Interview with Tony Leung', *Senses of Cinema* vol. 13 (April–May 2001), http://sensesofcinema.com/2001/wong-kar-wai/leung/, accessed 23 November 2015.

McDonald, Paul, 'Why Study Film Acting? Some Opening Reflections', in Cynthia Baron, Diane Carson and Frank P. Tomasulo (eds), *More than a Method: Trends and Traditions in Contemporary Film Performance* (Detroit Wayne State University Press, 2004), pp. 23–41.

Moy, Patsy, 'What the Chinese Government Did on June 4 Was Right – To Maintain Stability', *South China Morning Post*, 17 December 2002, http://www.scmp.com/article/400991/what-chinese-government-did-june-4-was-right-maintain-stability, accessed 2 May 2017.

Naremore, James, *Acting in the Cinema* (Berkeley: University of California Press, 1988).

Neale, Steve, 'Art Cinema as Institution', *Screen* vol. 22 no. 1 (March 1981), pp. 11–39.

Nochimson, Martha P., 'Lies and Loneliness: An Interview with Tony Leung Chiu Wai', *Cineaste* vol. 30 no. 4 (Fall 2005), pp. 16–17.

O'Dell, Leslie, *The Charismatic Chameleon: The Actor as Creative Artist* (Portland, OR: Sussex Academic Press, 2010).

Oon, Clarissa, 'Chinese Bacall and Bogart', *Straits Times* (Singapore), 22 January 2003. Reprinted at http://www.tonyleung.info/news/interview2003_2.shtml, accessed 20 November 2015.

Rawnsley, Gary D. and Ming-Yeh T. Rawnsley (eds), *Global Chinese Cinema: The Culture and Politics of Hero* (London: Routledge, 2010).

Rayns, Tony, 'Deep Cover', *Sight and Sound*, January 2004, http://old.bfi.
  org.uk/sightandsound/feature/29, accessed 23 November 2015.

Reich, Jacqueline, *Beyond the Latin Lover: Marcello Mastroianni, Masculinity,
  and Italian Cinema* (Bloomington: Indiana University Press, 2004).

Reynaud, Berenice, 'Entretien avec Wong Kar-Wai', *Cahiers du Cinéma* vol.
  490 (April 1995), pp. 37–9.

Rose, Steve, '"It Never Gets Any Easier," Tony Leung', *China
  Daily*, 23 February 2004, http://www.chinadaily.com.cn/english/
  doc/2004-05/19/content_331961.htm, accessed 23 November 2015.

Seno, Alexandra A., 'Asia's Moody Hero', *Newsweek*, 24 February 2003.
  Reprinted at http://www.tonyleung.info/news/interview2003_1.shtml,
  accessed 23 November 2015.

Serpytyte, Agne, 'City of Sadness' (film review), *Asian Cinema Blog*,
  21 April 2015, http://theasiancinemablog.com/taiwan-cinema/
  city-of-sadness-movie-review/, accessed 8 June 2016.

Siegel, Marc, 'The Intimate Spaces of Wong Kar-Wai', in Esther C. M.
  Yau (ed.), *At Full Speed: Hong Kong Cinema in a Borderless World*
  (Minneapolis: University of Minnesota Press, 2001), pp. 277–94.

Shin, Chi-Yun, 'Double Identity: The Stardom of Xun Zhou and the Figure
  of the Femme Fatale', in Chi-Yun Shin and Mark Gallagher (eds), *East
  Asian Film Noir* (London: I. B. Tauris, 2015), pp. 215–31.

Song, Geng and Derek Hird, *Men and Masculinities in Contemporary China*
  (Leiden: Brill, 2013).

Springer, Claudia, 'Introduction', in Claudia Springer and Julie Levinson
  (eds), *Acting* (New Brunswick, NJ: Rutgers University Press, 2015),
  pp. 1–24.

St Michel, Patrick, 'Japanese Demons and Crotch Bombs: The Tense
  State of Asian Cinema', *The Atlantic*, 9 September 2015, http://www.
  theatlantic.com/entertainment/archive/2015/09/east-asian-films-wwii-
  anniversary/404152/, accessed 23 December 2015.

Stokes, Lisa Odham, *Historical Dictionary of Hong Kong Cinema* (Lanham,
  MD: Scarecrow Press, 2007).

Sun, Shaoyi, 'Trends in Chinese Cinema, Part II – Trend One: Playing the
  "Main Melody"', *Shaoyi Sun's Film Review Blog*, 1 April 2010, https://
  shaoyis.wordpress.com/2010/04/01/trends-in-chinese-cinema-part-ii/,
  accessed 8 June 2016.

Sun, Shaoyi, 'Top 10 Box Office Films of 2012 in China', *Shaoyi Sun's Film Review Blog*, 6 January 2013, http://shaoyis.wordpress.com/2013/01/06/top-10-box-office-films-of-2012-in-china/, accessed 10 June 2013.

Szeto, Mirana M. and Yun-Chung Chen, 'Mainlandization or Sinophone Translocality? Challenges for Hong Kong SAR New Wave Cinema', *Journal of Chinese Cinemas* vol. 6 no. 2 (2012), pp. 115–34.

Szeto, Mirana M. and Yun-Chung Chen, 'To Work or Not to Work: The Dilemma of Hong Kong Film Labor in the Age of Mainlandization', *Jump Cut* vol. 55 (Fall 2013), www.ejumpcut.org/currentissue/SzetoChenHongKong/index.html, accessed 22 January 2014.

Teo, Stephen, *Wong Kar-Wai* (London: BFI Publishing, 2005).

Teo, Stephen, 'Film Genre and Chinese Cinema: A Discourse of Film and Nation', in Yingjin Zhang (ed.), *A Companion to Chinese Cinema* (Malden, MA: Blackwell, 2012), pp. 284–98.

Tong, Kelvin, 'A Star Is Born Again', *Straits Times* (Singapore), 4 November 2000. Reprinted at http://tonyleung.info/news/straits.shtml, accessed 12 June 2014.

'Tony Leung Almost "Dies" after Hearing His Voice Dubbing', *Apple Daily* (Taiwan), 2013, http://appledaily.com.tw. Reprinted at *Asianpopnews.com*, 14 January, http://asianpopnews.com/tony-leung-almost-dies-after-hearing-his-voice-dubbing/, accessed 7 January 2016.

'Tony Leung Chiu-Wai Claims He Was Misquoted Regarding Tiananmen', *Hong Kong Entertainment News in Review*, 19 December 2002, http://www.hkentreview.com/2002/december/decother/tltian.html, accessed 5 June 2007.

'Tony Leung Chiu-Wai: Sexiest Newcomer', *People*, 13 November 2000, http://people.com/archive/tony-leung-chiu-wai-sexiest-newcomer-vol-54-no-20/, accessed 28 August 2017.

'Tony's Music Album', *tonyleung.info*, n.d., http://www.tonyleung.info/multimedia/music.shtml, accessed 29 October 2015.

Turner, Matthew, 'Hong Kong Sixties/Nineties: Dissolving the People', in Matthew Turner and Irene Ngan (eds), *Hong Kong Sixties: Designing Identity* (Hong Kong: Hong Kong Arts Center, 1995), pp. 13–34.

Tweedie, James, *The Age of New Waves: Art Cinema and the Staging of Globalization* (New York: Oxford University Press, 2013).

Wang, Yiman, 'Watching Anna May Wong in Republican China', in Lisa Funnell and Man-Fung Yip (eds), *American and Chinese-Language Cinemas: Examining Cultural Flows* (New York: Routledge, 2015), pp. 169–85.

Weinstein Company, The, 'The Grandmaster: Production Notes', 2013, http://www.twcpublicity.com/movie.php?id=174#production, accessed 11 November 2015.

Wilkinson, James, 'Tony Leung: Star of The Great Magician Talks to Time Out', *Time Out Beijing*, 2 January 2012, http://www.timeoutbeijing.com/features/Books__Film/14172/Tony-Leung.html, accessed 7 June 2013.

Williams, Tony, 'Tony Leung Chiu-Wai', in Gary Bettinson (ed.), *Directory of World Cinema: China 2* (Bristol: Intellect, 2015), pp. 57–60.

Wong, Eugene Franklin, *On Visual Media Racism: Asians in the American Motion Pictures* (New York: Arno Press, 1978).

Wong, Martin and Nakamura, Eric, 'Tony Leung' (interview), *Giant Robot* vol. 21 (2001), pp. 32–5, 86. Reprinted at http://www.tonyleung.info/news/giant1.shtml, accessed 23 November 2015.

Yip, Man-Fung, 'Martial Arts Cinema and Minor Transnationalism', in Lisa Funnell and Man-Fung Yip (eds), *American and Chinese-Language Cinemas: Examining Cultural Flows* (New York: Routledge, 2015), pp. 86–100.

Yu, Sabrina Qiong, 'Jet Li: Star Construction and Fan Discourse on the Internet', in Mary Farquhar and Yingjin Zhang (eds), *Chinese Film Stars* (New York: Routledge, 2010), pp. 225–36.

Yu, Sabrina Qiong, *Jet Li: Chinese Masculinity and Transnational Film Stardom* (Edinburgh: Edinburgh University Press, 2012a).

Yu, Sabrina Qiong, 'Vulnerable Chinese Stars: From *Xizi* to Film Worker', in Yingjin Zhang (ed.), *A Companion to Chinese Cinema* (Malden, MA: Blackwell, 2012b), pp. 218–38.

Zhang, Rui, *The Cinema of Feng Xiaogang: Commercialization and Censorship in Chinese Cinema after 1989* (Hong Kong: Hong Kong University Press, 2008).

Zhang, Yinglin and Mary Farquhar, 'Introduction: Chinese Film Stars', in Yinglin Zhang and Mary Farquhar (eds), *Chinese Film Stars* (London: Routledge, 2010), pp. 1–16.

Zito, Angela and Tani E. Barlow (eds), *Body, Subject, and Power in China* (Chicago University of Chicago Press, 1994).

# FILMOGRAPHY

Note: The following list includes the films' and series' most common
English titles, with alternate English and Cantonese titles in brackets
(or for some co-productions, Mandarin or Vietnamese titles). Film titles,
release years and director and character names are cross-referenced
from the Internet Movie Database (www.imdb.com), the Hong Kong
Movie Database (www.hkmdb.com), and Hong Kong Cinemagic
(www.hkcinemagic.com).

## Films

MAD, MAD 83 [aka *Feng kuang ba san*] (Chor Yuen, Hong Kong,
    1983), character name unknown.
FASCINATING AFFAIRS [aka *Hua xin hong xing*] (Alfred Cheung,
    Chor Yuen and Wong Jing, Hong Kong, 1985), Kit.
YOUNG COPS [aka *Qing chun chai guan*] (Yau Kar-Hung, Hong Kong,
    1985), Leung Siu-Bo.
THE LUNATICS [aka *Din lo jing juen*] (Yee Tung-Shing, Hong Kong,
    1986), Doggie.
LOVE UNTO WASTE [aka *Love Unto Wastes* and *Dei ha ching*] (Stanley
    Kwan, Hong Kong, 1986), Tony Cheung.
HAPPY-GO-LUCKY [aka *Kai xin kuai huo ren*] (Lee Tim-Sing, Hong
    Kong, 1987), Wei.
PEOPLE'S HERO [aka *Yan man ying hung*] (Yee Tung-Shing, Hong
    Kong, 1987), Sai.

I LOVE MARIA [aka *Tie jia wu di Ma Li Ya*] (David Chung, Hong Kong, 1988), T. Q. Zhuang.

TWO PAINTERS [aka *Sha shou hu die meng*] (Yu Kan Ping, Hong Kong, 1989), character name unknown.

MY HEART IS THAT ETERNAL ROSE [aka *Sha shou hu die meng*] (Patrick Tam, Hong Kong, 1989), Cheung.

SEVEN WARRIORS [aka *Zhong yi qun ying*] (Sammo Hung and Terry Tong, Hong Kong, 1989), Wong Way-Wu.

A CITY OF SADNESS [aka *Bei qing cheng shi*] (Hou Hsiao-Hsien, Hong Kong/Taiwan, 1989), Wen-Ching.

BULLET IN THE HEAD [aka *Dip huet gaai tau*] (John Woo, Hong Kong, 1990), Ben/Ah Bee.

DAYS OF BEING WILD [aka *Ah Fei zing zyun*] (Wong Kar-Wai, Hong Kong, 1990), Chow Mo-Wan.

THE ROYAL SCOUNDREL [aka *Sa tan zai jyu zau si nai*] (Chik Ki Yee and Johnnie To, Hong Kong, 1991), Beach Boy.

DON'T FOOL ME [aka *Chung Waan ying hung*] (Herman Yau, Hong Kong, 1991), Chiang Ho-Chie.

FANTASY ROMANCE [aka *Moh wah ching*] (Taylor Wong, Hong Kong, 1991), Shing.

THE GREAT PRETENDERS [aka *Qian wang 1991*] (Ronny Yu, Hong Kong, 1991), Snake Wai.

THE TIGERS [aka *Gam paai ng foo cheung*] (Eric Tsang, Hong Kong, 1991), Tau-Pi.

A CHINESE GHOST STORY III [aka *Sien lui yau wan III: Do do do*] (Ching Siu-Tung, Hong Kong, 1991), Fong.

THE BANQUET [aka *Ho moon ye yin*] (Alfred Cheung, Cheung Tung Cho, Clifton Ko and Tsui Hark, Hong Kong, 1991), Wai Chai.

COME FLY THE DRAGON [aka *Hei yi bu zhi Shou du qing shen*] (Eric Tsang, Hong Kong, 1992), Liu Chia-Lun.

LUCKY ENCOUNTER [aka *Tek dou bou*] (Johnnie To, Hong Kong, 1992), Dian Fa.

THE DAYS OF BEING DUMB [aka *Ah Fei yue Ah Kei*] (Blackie Ko Shou Liang, Hong Kong, 1992), Fred Tung.

HARD-BOILED [aka *Lat sau san taam*] (John Woo, Hong Kong, 1992), Tony/Alan.

THREE SUMMERS [aka *Ge ge de qing ren*] (Lawrence Ah Mon, Hong Kong, 1992), Wai.

THE MAGIC CRANE [aka *Xin xian he shen zhen*] (Benny Chan, Hong Kong, 1993), Ma Kwun-Mo.

END OF THE ROAD [aka *Yi yu zhi mo lu ying xiong*] (Chu Yen-Ping, Taiwan, 1993), Fan Long.

BUTTERFLY AND SWORD [aka *San lau sing woo dip gim*] (Michael Mak, Hong Kong, 1993), Meng Sing-Wan.

TOM, DICK AND HAIRY [aka *Feng chen san xia*] (Peter Chan Ho-Sun, Hong Kong, 1993), Tom Chan.

HERO – BEYOND THE BOUNDARY OF TIME [aka *Wei Xiao Bao: Feng zhi gou nu*] (Blackie Ko Shou Liang, Hong Kong, 1993), Wai Siu-Bo.

THE EAGLE SHOOTING HEROES [aka *Se diu ying hung ji dung sing sai jau*] (Jeffrey Lau, Hong Kong, 1993), Ou-Yang Feng.

TWO OF A KIND [aka *Qing ren zhi ji*] (Teddy Chen Tak-Sum, Hong Kong, 1993), Lam Dai-Chi.

HE AIN'T HEAVY, HE'S MY FATHER [aka *San naam hing naan dai*] (Peter Chan Ho-Sun, Hong Kong, 1994), Chu Yuan.

ALWAYS BE THE WINNERS [aka *Shen long du sheng zhi qi kai de sheng*] (Jacky Pang Yee-Wah, Hong Kong, 1994), Third Master Sha.

THE RETURNING [aka *Dang chuek lei wooi loi*] (Cheung Chi Leung, Hong Kong, 1994), Lee Yick-Chung.

CHUNGKING EXPRESS [aka *Chung Hing sam lam*] (Wong Kar-Wai, Hong Kong, 1994), Officer 663.

ASHES OF TIME [aka *Dung che sai duk*] (Wong Kar-Wai, Hong Kong/ Taiwan, 1994), Blind Swordsman.

TOMORROW [aka *Iron Butterfly III: Tomorrow, Dak ging 90 III: Zi ming jat tin ngaai* and *Ming yat tin aai*] (Johnnie To, Hong Kong, 1995 TV movie), character name unknown.

HEAVEN CAN'T WAIT [aka *Gau sai san gwan*] (Lee Chi-Ngai, Hong Kong, 1995), Wong Tai-Fung.

CYCLO [aka *Xich lô*] (Tran Anh Hung, Vietnam/France/Hong Kong, 1995), Poet.

WAR OF THE UNDERWORLD [aka *Xong xing zi: Zhi jiang hu da feng bao*] (Herman Yau, Hong Kong, 1996), Hong Fei.

BLIND ROMANCE [aka *Tau tau oi nei*] (Tam Long-Cheung, Hong Kong, 1996), Wing.

'97 ACES GO PLACES [aka *Jui gaai paak dong ji: Jui gaai paak dong*] (Chin Kar-Lok, Hong Kong, 1997), Chui Cheong/Drunk Gun.

HAPPY TOGETHER [aka *Chun gwong cha sit*] (Wong Kar-Wai, Hong Kong/Japan/South Korea, 1997), Lai Yiu-Fai.

CHINESE MIDNIGHT EXPRESS [aka *Hak yuk duen cheung goh: Chai sang jue yuk*] (Billy Tang, Hong Kong, 1997), Ahn.

DR. MACK [aka *Mack the Knife* and *Lau man yi sang*] (Lee Chi-Ngai, Hong Kong, 1998, Dr Lau Mack.

THE LONGEST NITE [aka *Am faa*] (Patrick Yau, Hong Kong, 1998), Sam.

TIMELESS ROMANCE [aka *Chiu si hung yiu oi*] (David Lai and Jeffrey Lau, Hong Kong, 1998), Lau Yat Lo/Zhuge Liang.

YOUR PLACE OR MINE [aka *Mooi tin oi lei 8 siu see*] (James Yuen, Hong Kong, 1998), Wai.

FLOWERS OF SHANGHAI [aka *Hai shang hua*] (Hou Hsiao-Hsien, Taiwan/Japan, 1998), Wang.

GORGEOUS [aka *Boh lei chun*] (Vincent Kok, Hong Kong/Taiwan, 1999), Albert.

HEALING HEARTS [aka *Hap gwat yan sam*] (Gary Tang, Hong Kong, 2000), Dr Lawrence Ching.

IN THE MOOD FOR LOVE [aka *Hua yang nian hua*] (Wong Kar-Wai, Hong Kong, 2000), Chow Mo-Wan.

TOKYO RAIDERS [aka *Dong jing gong lüe*] (Jingle Ma, Hong Kong, 2000), Lin.

LOVE ME, LOVE MY MONEY [aka *Yau ching yam shui baau*] (Wong Jing, Hong Kong, 2001), Richard Ma.

FIGHTING FOR LOVE [aka *Tung gui mat yau*] (Joe Ma, Hong Kong, 2001), Tung-Choi.

CHINESE ODYSSEY 2002 [aka *Tian xia wu shuang*] (Jeffrey Lau, Hong Kong, 2002), Li Yilong.

HERO [aka *Ying xiong*] (Zhang Yimou, Hong Kong/China, 2002), Broken Sword.

INFERNAL AFFAIRS [aka *Mou gaan dou*] (Andrew Lau and Alan Mak, Hong Kong, 2002), Chan Wing Yan.

MY LUCKY STAR [aka *Hung wun chiu yun*] (Vincent Kok, Hong Kong, 2003), Lai Liu Po.

INFERNAL AFFAIRS III [aka *Mou gaan dou III: Jung gik mou gaan*] (Andrew Lau and Alan Mak, Hong Kong/China, 2003), Chan Wing Yan.

SOUND OF COLORS [aka *Dei ha tit*] (Joe Ma, Hong Kong, 2003), Ming.

2046 (Wong Kar-Wai, Hong Kong/China/France/Italy/Germany, 2004), Chow Mo-Wan.

SEOUL RAIDERS [aka *Hon shing gung leuk*] (Jingle Ma, South Korea/ Hong Kong, 2005), Lam.

CONFESSION OF PAIN [aka *Seung sing*] (Andrew Lau and Alan Mak, Hong Kong, 2006), Lau Ching Hei.

LUST, CAUTION [aka *Se, jie*] (Ang Lee, US/China/Taiwan, 2007), Mr Yee.

RED CLIFF [aka *Chi bi*] (John Woo, China/Hong Kong/Japan/Taiwan/ South Korea, 2008), Zhou Yu.

ASHES OF TIME REDUX [aka *Dung che sai duk redux*] (Wong Kar-Wai, Hong Kong/Taiwan, 2008), Blind Swordsman.

RED CLIFF II [*aka Chi bi: Jue zhan tian xia*] (John Woo, China/Hong Kong/Japan/Taiwan/South Korea, 2009), Zhou Yu.

THE GREAT MAGICIAN [aka *Daai mo seut si*] (Yee Tung-Shing, Hong Kong/China, 2011), Zhang Xian.

THE SILENT WAR [aka *Ting feng zhe*] (Felix Chong and Alan Mak, Hong Kong/China, 2012), He Bing.

THE GRANDMASTER [aka *Yat doi zung si*] (Wong Kar Wai, Hong Kong/China, 2013), Ip Man.

HEMA HEMA: SING ME A SONG WHILE I WAIT (Khyentse Norbu, Bhutan/Hong Kong, 2016), Deer/Serene Mask.

SEE YOU TOMORROW [aka *Bai du ren*] (Zhang Jiajia, Hong Kong/ China, 2016), Chen Mo.

# Television series

**Note:** director credits not available; station names in parentheses

THE YOUNG HEROES OF SHAOLIN [aka *Ying xiong chu shao nian*] (TVB, Hong Kong, 1981), character name unknown (Shaolin monk).

THE LEGEND OF MASTER SO [aka *Su qi er*] (TVB, Hong Kong, 1981), character name unknown (waiter).

DEMI-GODS AND SEMI-DEVILS [aka *Tin lung baat bou*] (TVB, Hong Kong, 1981 or 1982), character name unknown (monk).

MANAGER & MESSENGER [aka *Manager and Office Boy* and *Jing li hou sheng*] (TVB, Hong Kong, 1981 or 1982), character name unknown (General Manager's son).

HONG KONG '82 [aka *Xiang gang ba er*] (TVB, Hong Kong, 1982), character name unknown.

430 SPACE SHUTTLE [aka *Chuan suo ji*] (TVB, Hong Kong, 1982–9 [with Leung appearing circa 1982]), character name unknown (presenter).

SOLDIER OF FORTUNE [aka *Heung sing long ji*] (TVB, Hong Kong, 1982), Ying Chi-Him.

LONELY GENIUS [aka *Dynamic Eleven* and *Wut lik sap jat*] (TVB, Hong Kong, 1983), Hung Kwok-Choi.

THE EMISSARY [aka *Lie ying*] (TVB, Hong Kong, 1982–3), Ying Chi-Him.

THE SUPERPOWER [aka *Tian jiang cai shen*] (TVB, Hong Kong, 1983), Kwok Hak-Chung.

FAREWELL 19 [aka *Beyond the Rose Garden*, *Choi kin sap kau sui* and *Zai jian shi jiu sui*] (TVB, Hong Kong, 1983), Ma Tin-Yau.

ENCOUNTER WITH FORTUNE [aka *Lucky Ghost* and *Gui gan gou yun*] (TVB, Hong Kong, 1983), character name unknown.

ANGELS AND DEVILS [aka *But dou san hung*] (TVB, Hong Kong, 1983), Kong Ho-Man.

NO REGRETS FOR OUR YOUTH [aka *Wo dui qing chun wu hui*] (TVB, Hong Kong, 1983), Frankie.

CROSSROADS [aka *Lin qi*] (RTHK, Hong Kong, 1983), Ah Man.

THE CLONES [aka *The Replica* and *Zai ban ren*] (TVB, Hong Kong, 1984), Cheung Ka-Wai.

THE DUKE OF MOUNT DEER [aka *Luk ding gei*] (TVB, Hong Kong, 1984), Wai Siu-Bo.

IT'S A LONG WAY HOME [aka *Ga yao gui chai*] (TVB, Hong Kong, 1984), Yau Ga-Kei.

POLICE CADET [aka *Police Cadet '84* and *San jaat si hing*] (TVB, Hong Kong, 1984), Cheung Wai-Kit.

POLICE CADET '85 [aka *San jaat si hing: juk jaap*] (TVB, Hong Kong, 1985), Cheung Wai-Kit.

THE ROUGH RIDE [aka *Tiao zhan*] (TVB, Hong Kong, 1985), Chow Kim-Hung.

THE YANG'S SAGA [aka *The Yangs' Saga* and *Yang ka cheung*] (TVB, Hong Kong, 1985), Yang Chuk-Long.

THE NEW HEAVEN SWORD AND DRAGON SABRE [aka *New Heavenly Sword and Dragon Sabre, The Heaven Sword and Dragon Saber* and *Yi tian tu long ji*] (TVB, Hong Kong, 1986), Cheung Mo-Kei.

THE GRAND CANAL [aka *Da yun*] (TVB, Hong Kong, 1987), Cheung Sam-Long.

POLICE CADET '88 [aka *San jaat si hing 88*] (TVB, Hong Kong, 1988), Cheung Wai-Kit.

TWO MOST HONORABLE KNIGHTS [aka *Chut toi sheung kiu*] (TVB, Hong Kong, 1988), Kong Siu-Yu.

BEHIND SILK CURTAINS [aka *Da du hui*] (TVB, Hong Kong, 1988), Lin Kar-Yip.

THE SEASONS [aka *Ji jie*] (TVB, Hong Kong, 1988), Sam-Dee.

CITY FORMULA [aka *Everybody's Somebody's Favorite* and *Du shi fang cheng shi*] (TVB, Hong Kong, 1989), character name unknown.

ODE TO GALLANTRY [aka *Hap hak hang*] (TVB, Hong Kong, 1989), Shek Po-Tin/Shek Chung-Yuk.

# INDEX

**Note:** Page numbers in **bold** indicate detailed analysis; those in *italic* denote illustrations. *n* = endnote.